Fighting Fashion

Helen Storey was born in Belsize Park, London, in 1959.
The daughter of playwright and novelist David Storey, she
was educated at Hampstead Comprehensive and studied
fashion design at Kingston Polytechnic. She worked in
Italy for Valentino and Lancetti in the early 1980s, and after
three years returned to start her own label. She has won
awards for both innovation and export and has sold her
collections to twenty-four countries throughout the world
and to many celebrities.

Helen Storey

Fighting Fashion

ff

faber and faber

First published in 1996
by Faber and Faber Limited
3 Queen Square London WC1N 3AU

Typeset by Faber and Faber Ltd
Printed in England by Clays Ltd, St Ives plc

© Helen Storey, 1996

Helen Storey is hereby identified as author of this
work in accordance with Section 77 of the Copyright,
Designs and Patents Act 1988

A CIP record for this book
is available from the British Library

ISBN 0–571–17973–8

10 9 8 7 6 5 4 3 2 1

Contents

'I find there is a natural opposition in men for anything they haven't thought of for themselves – do you find that?

BARNES-WALLACE

Little Red Riding
Hood, 1964

Helen
22/2/64

There are three elements which ensure that fashion is the only place for me. The first is my knowledge of the female form, both self-informed and slapped into me in detail through eleven years of ballet. The second is my love of cloth's instruction. And last there is my addiction to the evolving psyche of women.

Beyond the eyes of men, and of any female state that is named – mother, lover, worker, wife – my creativity is my difference. I cannot resist starting again, as if in rediscovering the possibility of a creative new, I am on some level reaffirming that I exist.

For Luke

1

Back to Lyndhurst

In the past I might have flung on any number of things as appropriate to the Downing Street invitation, but it will need more thought this time. I have been sitting in an armchair for months. Throughout the winter I have sat quite still and am too familiar with the red brickwork of the house opposite my window. I have given up chasing the cats that crap on my sleeping garden. The guests will wear seventies-looking shoes, Gucci tabards and hairdos which hover and stay.

Now in my mid-thirties, everything has changed. What does it feel like when the need to run has gone? The driven part of me, the part that plunged into creating the Helen Storey name, that couldn't wait to leave my miserable education behind, to be in control, of something maybe even further back than that, has gone. And during the time designated for me to come back and relaunch, fate and my need for stillness have precluded both. I now deal in the small, in the detail of pennies rather than the rounding up of thousands. I am down to collecting premier points from that supermarket and Income Support of £25 per week.

It's during the day that I miss the part of me I thought I knew. Eleven a.m. in my local superstore is the magical time. The employed are away in offices somewhere. Mothers have their young to push ahead of them. And then there is me, and the rest of the long-term unemployed. I can tell you that Andrex is £1.22 more expensive than Somerfield's basic-range toilet tissue, that when I am feeling self-destructive you will find me shopping in Food Giant, and that a local shop whose largest sign in the window says 'Convert your jukebox' has a business that has survived longer than mine did.

Every piece of post is expected, yet this period is about nothing definite. It is a passing-through, a leaving-behind – a bungee jump on the inside. In the spirit of my friends Richard and Graham, you could say I am working towards my freedom. You catch me, however, tossing my head violently from side to side, an old bone locked tight in my jaws. Spit flies and I growl beyond my known nature. I am not wrestling with failure; I am confronting my former omnipotence, the all-powerful part of me that created a label now no longer in existence. I can shed it, drop it or hold on to it. It's taken months, but with not a design in sight, I can see my next season. It is smaller, a bit here, a bit there, no frills – not for profit alone, but a backable venture into me. It could be a play: a divided stage, backstage revealed, the catwalk out into the audience. I know the dialogue, the way we do it, but I still question the reason as to why. I have designed the set, know the cast is of twenty, can sense which theatre and recognize that in this play lies the stuff of my dancing and my years in fashion.

In my cupboard I have an old tabard. It is acid yellow and embroidered with diamante up the back. If you wear it back to front, it gives you the best-shaped breasts. With some boots left over from my last collection and my long hair I just might, with a push, hover and stay.

Something in the mountain's colossal and bold permanence challenged me to climb. The thought came to me while walking in Wales with a group of friends a year ago that I am drawn towards those things in life that I imagine will never change. Lyndhurst, though now gone, is one such place.

In 1960 my father won a prize for a novel he touted round thirteen different publishers before it was finally accepted. My birth and critical acclaim for *This Sporting Life* happened at around the same time. With the prize money my parents bought a cream Mark-2 Jaguar, a living-room on wheels and relief from the two rooms in Bloomsbury we all shared. I would sit on the back seat, aged one, while my father went flat-hunting. The trail ended at 2 Lyndhurst Gardens, just above Belsize Village.

I don't have a first memory. In its place was a slow and creeping realization of a broader picture coming into focus. I don't recall ever being the only one, though at times, being the oldest of four, I must have experienced much as if I was. Over the years I have often felt a strong urge to take people back to Lyndhurst, my nostalgia for the place – all the more poignant because it no longer exists.

It was dark – a huge house, split quite naturally into three flats. The servants' quarters and basement were ours. The middle flat belonged to a childless Swedish couple called Dan and Elsa, and at the top lived a short, pretty pigeon of a woman called Midge. In later years, through either greed or a con, she sold out to developers and the whole lot was knocked to the ground. A small block of yellow-brick flats took its place.

Stone steps worn smooth and at odd angles led a path under the house to a bunker on the left and our front door and a bathroom window on the right. Entering the hall through a door consistently on the latch, there was only ever borrowed light from the rooms beyond. The square hall had no windows but

My caterpillar, aged 3

five entrances which led to the rest of the flat. Bedrooms moved constantly as one child became four and girls and boys grew apart.

My brothers, Jake and Sean, shared a back room off the living-room with a metal Shakespeare knocker on the outside of the door. The windows looked out to the foreign territory of the garden belonging to the upstairs tenants. My sister and I eventually shared an old billiard room with a hand-scrolled ceiling in cream plaster. In our palms a roaring brass lion's-head left its mark as we twisted it to open the door, revealing two beautifully carved and curved wooden steps into the room itself. On the right-hand wall wild and giant white cabbages flaked on to bottle-green background, and french windows opened on to the limer green of the garden outside. The floors throughout the house were of bare varnished wood.

It was a hide-and-seek palace. Coats and wellingtons bulged as dead bodies, faces turned to the wall, perfect camouflage from which to burst, terrifying

Luke's caterpillar, aged 4

another sibling. We seemed to take it in turns to have an accident before reaching a raised lavatory at the end. Cupboards were big enough to lie in and triumphant 'ha-has' were the communal cry of any rainy day indoors.

My father worked at home. He left once to try it elsewhere but came back. He travelled between two people: father and writer. His two worlds met in the ritual of 'first nights'; the staging of plays – often written in a number of days – was where he confronted the outside world. Much of my childhood fathoming of him was experienced through evenings at the Royal Court Theatre. A mixture of feelings surfaced each time, differing in intensity, my own age determining a changing response over the years. In contrast to his own unease, overwhelmingly, pride was my instinctive reaction. To see the work momentarily in the public arena and not his room made some much-needed sense of the times when, as a young girl, I perceived he went missing from the world. His work often shocked me. The swearing, so undesirable in our home and on occasions so blatant in his writing, a sense of humour and of people which I came to understand in later plays, were only fully appreciated as an adult. As a child, I often felt jealous or left out of a process which, while defining him so completely, was one I could never play a part in. As a daughter on these nights, it was as much the response of others to him as a presence that caught my attention as it was any reaction to the plays themselves. Despite the constant partnership of my glamorous, proud and supportive mother, it was the other women who were drawn to him that early on introduced the idea of him as a man independent of his role as my father. I never quite made sense of the agony, thinking 'first nights' such a temporary pay-off. I didn't understand then. The act of writing was enough.

I fought often with my younger sister, Kate. Some days I would draw a chalk line down the middle of our room, the rule being that her mess stayed north of my neatened south. Constant permission to cross my domain was asked of me as the south side had the advantage of the only door. As children, we fought and played hard. Indoors meant rain, grey skies and uncontrollable noise. Happiness was to treat the flat as an

Linocut Dad used for the programme of his play *The Changing Room*

Red Indian, 1964

obstacle course: to open the kitchen's second door and link it with speed to the bathroom corridor, a tight time-limit being applied to these circuits of joy. Revenge was to find something loved by or precious to another and drop it down the cracks in the floorboards – a Nancy Sinatra 45 slipped through perfectly.

There seemed to be more children in the sixties – great gangs of them. Even dogs had mates. They would call at each other's houses, barking to announce another Enid Blyton adventure in the offing. An ugly bunch, they roamed with authority, knowing all the short-cuts around the village, their carefree bravado not dissimilar to our own.

Johnny was supposed to be a hamster. Jake and my father had gone to a pet shop in Parkway, Camden Town, to put an end to Jake's nagging for one. When Johnny arrived, he was in fact a cute but soon to be sick puppy; his cheap price gave no clue to the eventual cost of keeping him alive. My mother stayed up nights, nursing him as a newborn. At first he was loved fairly well by all, but as his body grew and his legs and head stayed the same, there was a slow shifting of backs (and responsibility) as his destined ugliness became apparent. His farts were triumphant and silent, and a wry smile would spread across his mottled and whiskered jaw, as if he considered all these qualities a virtue. Towards the end, as he had predicted, my father was Johnny's reluctant and only mate. As Johnny grew older and smellier, he developed cancer of the testicles and my father and Jake finally took him off to the village vet one day to have him put down. As in life, so in death: he rolled his pink-and-black lips back to smile at my father a last time, a thank-you for putting an end to the misery that had been the last few months of his life.

The village itself was small. From our house the alley down the side of the garden led first to the Kray brothers. The Krays ran the cobblers under the flat where they lived. They signalled every lunchtime by pulling half-window blackout curtains across wide and tall panes of glass. Unconsciously I monitored the change in my height against what I could increasingly see over their counter. I recall leaning out of my pram, running my hands over the corrugated but smooth hardboard, a bump and a recess every inch. I would strum the surface as we waited until my mother, shoes wrapped in newspaper, pushed us back up the alley. The air was full of heavy glue and the leather stained their hands and faces. One brother spoke – how the children had grown, the sun or lack of it – while the other polished in the background. They were tough, like the footwear they mended, yet gentle. I liked them. A timeless pair, waved at to and from home, they were there before we arrived and after we left – like the churches in the area, one every 500 yards: faith in those days, restoration now. Reebok times have made the Krays' craft redundant.

Around the corner, Monty had a shop he called a delicatessen that clung on to the traditional sort of food: Scott's Porridge Oats, baked beans and Heinz everything. The family had a tab there, my first experience of the word 'credit'. Babs ran the launderette, a glitzy woman who could have run something far more exciting and probably did. A centre of excitement was Conrad's Bistro, known then as the Witch's Cauldron. In the early days, Twiggy and David Bailey lived on the sloped crescent and spent much time there. Indian food arrived with scepticism at first, but the Beer-and-Curry house soon became a retreat – for parents needing breaks – a take-away – reminder that they were possible.

I was about seven the first time I saw a woman I consciously thought I might want to be – an independent lady, who took the world on on her own terms. She was always dashing from her front door to a waiting cab or back again. Wearing fur high-heels and a musky perfume, her hair was always half up or half down – a sort of caught-between-love look. In later years I saw her face again, somewhere between Sylvia Kristel and Ornella Muti. In sharp contrast to my mother, she had a mysterious life, seemingly devoid of men, but through my childhood eyes she was what I thought my womanhood might look like.

The village was three boomerangs touching in their middles around an island hardly ever used. On the last leg of one of them was a sweetshop, a tiny hovel that belonged to the man with a bump on his head, his bump as shiny and boiled as the things he sold. Fat jars stood shoulder to shoulder, uniform and bulky, their contents ready to be weighed. Courtesy of his shop, most of my early friendships could be identified by a particular taste. My longest friendship was with Jessica, a shy discovery of eyes and blonde hair over a garden wall, and when finally we spoke, cherry bitters and peardrops kept our mouths alive and full of numb sting. Our decisions were punctuated by sweets: whether to stay the night at hers or mine, to end the day or meet the next. It was a toss-up between our sisters, to incur either the wrath of hers or the interfering energy of mine.

Jessica's flat was similar to ours, a basement, with the same chances to feel the unlit. It was a 'pad' of great anger, expressed in the smallest of things. Using the expensive jam preserve instead of the cheaper Robinson's would bring forth shrill and shocking screams from Jessica's mother. A snapped tap in the new shower and again her loathing of the youngsters who disturbed her order would be exposed. Jessica's mother was an artist who drew beautifully, clearly, with single lines. Her room lay at the end of a narrow, black corridor, a space for her sanity and its painting. Jessica's father, a gentle and detached man who worked nights at a casino, lived behind a screen in the living-room. Their lives missed each other on purpose, a successful marriage between rage and passivity.

Biba was our Mecca, a teenage womb, and we would go there whenever we could. We sat for hours behind its blackened windows in Kensington High Street. 'Posing' on soft, fat sofas, I studied women: the Biba girls, the customers, the leopards, the stripes, red hair and black nails. Biba made me want to grow up fast, to earn, to spend, to buy a piece of the feeling I had when I was inside that shop. Like coming out of a nightclub into the drab of the day, the idea of facing my teens without it was unthinkable.

Years later, I heard that Jessica had had a breakdown and was in the Royal Free Hospital in Hampstead. I didn't visit and I should have. Within our friendship, had we ever agreed on what drives women insane, what pushes them over the edge? In our past, we had had moments the same. For a while it was school, a parallel shyness, Bowie, jacks, a sibling too close. Despite the years, I was rendered a coward – an illogical place in my mind, stuck in the infections of youth, feared that her state was a prophetic version of mine.

Elizabeth Taylor rode in our green Mini one day, driven by my dad; my mum was in a shiny, black Mercedes with Richard Burton. I was very young; I didn't understand why my parents didn't keep on going their separate ways. The prospect of these two as step-parents was more than acceptable to me. When my teens arrived, from about eleven, any interest in or entrancement with my father's world was dropped and the forging of my own took on its messy and prolonged determination. Memories before this time are sweet. Malcolm McDowell was funny and feisty and taught my sister and me how to whack a ball over a net. Ralph Richardson was my 'grandpa' when I went to see him play in *Home* on my birthday; he bowed up to our box and the audience turned in expectation of a Royal, only to see a grinning young girl and her father. Much of my grounding is the result of having a father who can spot the real and avoid the meaningless. My definition as a woman comes as much from him as it does from my mother, who in a quieter way acknowledged that women's lives were changing. My parents' stayed together, but I saw how none of the others did. My mother found satisfaction and happiness through her children, but I noticed how other mothers often found only anger and depression in theirs.

These times now make me think of light and dark, of happiness and sadness. Somehow, on the days when the sun found its way through our avoiding windows, I was of lighter heart. When it was dim and the distraction of our surroundings was no longer enough, I went inside myself. The emotional state of those around became the brightness.

Being the oldest, I was destined to feel everything first. As children, we used to sit four in the bath, taking it in turns to be at the front near the hot tap. That was where I liked it, passing the warmth back to the others. For it to be of any use to the youngest, Sean, usually at the end, the water would have to be almost unbearably hot on me. In the bath we named ourselves as meat: beef at the front, through pork and lamb to chicken at the back. We screamed with delight as our father's huge eyes and large hands took a break from writing and scared us to death through the bathroom window at the side.

In the now vanished climate of children playing safely on the streets, there was an escape from of the deeper, hidden family – of the inside – where we returned when the light faded. Outside we children could forget the darkness of our Lyndhurst homes – never places of hardship, yet full of the suggestion of tough times to come. Most of the parents I knew were

First self-portrait? 1964

self-employed and as such had to create their own futures.

Aged four, I started ballet in a church hall in Belsize Park. Aged six, my first performance outside, I was an orange flame, one of a series to come out of Pandora's box. The fire was three rows thick, a line of yellow flames, red and then orange. I remember the occasion more for the pain at the top of my legs. In the absence of Lycra, flickering was painful. Stuck in a box with farting Amanda and the other flames, we squatted most of the ballet on damp grass while Pandora impressed her parents up front.

The class grew and shrank from time to time but there existed a core team of 'wannabe' ballerinas whose varied shapes, talents and problems kept us together over a period of almost ten years. We had two teachers, Leonie Urdang and Ruth Silk.

Leonie Urdang was my first taskmaster in life. She had a warm, shiny smile that I only ever saw when parents came to pick up their young ones or any of us passed a grade. Once dropped off and parents gone, we were under her command. There was a hunger in her to find a glimpse of star quality in any of us and once she had, she would work on it, usually far harder than our limbs could stand. The 'star' in me was to be able to hold my left leg *à la second* to my left cheek. In Adrianne it was the *derrière* and in Philippa it was to hold a position anywhere you bloody well wanted it.

Towards the end of *barre* work, we would get down on our backs to 'do' frogs: with our knees drawn up and then spread out to the sides, an amphibian offering of young genitals to the ceiling. Leonie would walk down the rows pushing backs into the floor and using her feet or hands to nudge the sides of knees flat to the surfaces. In moments of agony the thought that my parents paid for this sprang to mind. Those who cried were noted and silently slumped down the ranks. Eventually, I managed to splay myself flat and any extra pressure from above had no effect, as my thighs already lay neat next to the wood.

The classes were hard. No sooner had you grasped one step than another was introduced. Clearly there was a part of me which rose to the challenge of learning, but it was a close-run thing between survival and love of the dance itself. The classes ended with improvisation or free movement. Using our teacher's face as a barometer of our talents, we barged around the hall: *grands jetés* in the name of Galena Samtsova, arabesques held too long as Antoinette Sibley and, flapping wildly at imagined windows, we tried to compete as Markova's Black Swan. Death was both prolonged and inevitable, necks straining in a frequent attempt to have our final moments witnessed. Love and Death were the favoured roles for young ballerinas, so comical, the imitation of two states yet to be experienced founded in parody and the imagined emotions of others. 'Remember, girls, never sit with your thighs on the bus seat, only the edge of your bottoms. Don't let those muscles turn to flab.' You could always spot our girls: having paid the fare for a seat on the bus, they hardly ever used it.

The church hall had a stage we rarely occupied. Instead, our dancing was done on the splinter-ridden floor. The hall was always grey and cold when we arrived. Gas fires hung high on walls. Our *Dad's Army* location had an old upright piano just under the stage. Neville sat at it playing when prompted by Leonie. He had a habit of rocking back and forth in between pieces and before he began to play. His flat palms stroked the length of his thighs in time to a silent beat. He brought with him a metronome in a briefcase filled with his music scores. Before each class he would place it at the end of the piano, angled like a camera. His music did him in. The rocking and stroking stopped when he began and a different persona appeared; stronger, this banger of keys and soft pusher of pedals kneaded the piano into sound. Towards the end of an exercise my eyes were drawn to his, torn between the physical relief of an ending for me and an anguish, as I felt his nervousness return, occasionally leading to tears. Never triggered by the tone of a piece, a mistake or its reprimand, the tears seeped out – an inner leak from a troubled part of himself. Although customary to applaud him at the end of a class, my palms rarely met.

As I passed through my grades, written up in *Dancing Times* as 'reminiscent of the young Berosova', to my great embarrassment my mother confirmed my progress by inscribing my hanger and costumes 'Helena Storeyoski'. Hung on my peg, these were sources of disbelief and ridicule to my friends and I received wry looks of suspicion from competitors who didn't know me. I figured that if I didn't speak and danced well, there was a slim chance I'd get away with it. To my mother's credit, her well-intentioned graffiti was a response to early rebellion on my part over identity. I had told her that Helen Storey was not a name which could ever sound famous. At the height of my potential I was upgraded to the private classes of Maria Fay and the company of a young Russian dancer called Nina. She danced in the same transported way that Neville played. Born deaf, she felt the music through vibrations in the floor. Between the two there was a notable alliance, Neville's torment expressed through what he could hear, Nina's by what she could not. The passion in Nina was not apparent in me, most settled when cast as a man or animal. Ballet was pink and I felt punk. The influence of Michael Clarke and Matthew Bourne yet to come, I could not muster the obligatory smile demanded by ballet. With the shaven heads and feather cuts of school, the culture of skinhead and hippie, it was hard to reconcile the blocked tap of my evenings on point.

Belsize Park wasn't Hampstead. It was a hopeful place in which to grow up. When I was twelve, Midge was offered money to sell the house for redevelopment. The incentive would be passed down in diluted form to my parents. They considered every alternative, including staying and keeping the place between themselves and another couple. In the end, though, as the result of another's greed, we moved from our flat to a house around the corner.

After we moved, Johnny the dog would go missing, only to be found running around the garden that now fronted the demolition site. My brother Jake went back one day to retrieve him. He climbed over the garden wall and looked through the free-standing french windows to the wreckage inside. Lying among the smashed and irreplaceable craftsmanship that had been our home lay the record stuffed down the boards years before: 'These boots are made for walkin'' . . . Start walkin'.

2

The

Sophie

Years

Sally and Sophie entertained on dining-hall tables, pushed-together stages during lunch hours. Theirs was a performance of Bette Midler duets, jokes I can't remember and a courage I was drawn to.

I gave Soph all my David Cassidy pictures and posters. She claimed that at the time I had had enough of the obsession, that I had realized it was hopeless, but with her I would rekindle it. Locked in her dark and tiny bedroom, we flopped down on bended knees, chins stretched upwards, crying and singing badly. We kissed that glossy paper poster matt, rarely disappointed that it pouted no return of lips. Ours was a devout hysteria. We went to see him once at Wembley Stadium, packed and perched high at the back. It had been a five-hour ordeal of waiting and pushing. Then, eight hours later, on a side of north London that was too far away from home, we screamed and gasped as a brilliant white suit walked on to the stage. Years of chaotic passion blasted free from our mouths. It was Tony Blackburn. An embarrassed numbness came over us: that upside-down face found on babies when both joy and tears fight for position. The best way of coping with it was to make out that our feelings for Tone were remarkably close to those we had for David.

At the end of the third year at Hampstead Comprehensive, Sally was yanked off to boarding school and the infamous sight of the two of them, arm-in-arm charges of the school's humour, was no more.

Hampstead Comprehensive wasn't: it was in Cricklewood, a bum of an area that even now I live far too near. The school was on two sites, separated by a concrete yard and netball courts. The front of the school was red-blackish brick, the bricks of private education, age and supposed trust. The back building sought to be modern, sixties- or seventies-looking. It was purpose-built and white, bearing no relation to its frontal sister. A tongue of modernity stuck out of the back of the old school building: an ill-maintained pond, once intended as a mini-nature reserve but abandoned, a puddle for crisp packets and defiant fag butts. Through its mismatched architecture it inadvertently symbolized the muddled identity of education at the time.

The school was divided into houses, named after famous people – Drake, Fleming, Chaucer, Newton, Hillary – the idea being that some of their great qualities might rub off on our motley crew. The Tower was where they kept the 'non-brights', the basically thick and disruptive. It was at the front of the school on its own fifth floor. No matter where you were in the school, you could hear them. Up there, I perceived teachers regularly lost hope. Down on the ground, however, among the quieter atmosphere of study, there was still the possibility of learning. The Tower's windows, come sun or rain, were constantly being opened to expel rulers, gobs of spit and picked-on girls' hair-slides, while the desperate cries of the teacher competed with the noise as they tried to refasten the windows.

I hovered between the troublesome 'thickos', as we called them, and the averagely bright kids. I was aware that I still had trouble learning. The art class was where I really wanted to be, walking past it frequently in the hope of being 'spotted'. Art never found its way on to my timetable (while I was having a double dose of cookery, others sketched plants or drew Biba girls, cartoon-style). I envied those grey, shiny, smudged inside fingers and Rapidograph pens.

Then there was RE – religious education. It was assumed that the world was Christian; moreover, we had Mr Chrome's version of it too. He was tall and skinny, about six foot four. His jacket and trousers shone at the knees and elbows, a synthetic gesture to how often he wore his dark uniform; a red V-necked tank-top, a white shirt and a slim tie completed the ensemble. He always looked the same. His hair was oiled viciously to one side and the parting was razor-sharp. He had a slight stoop and always entered the class after we were all seated, poking his head around the door to make sure his flock were waiting. 'Good morning, class,' and down would go his briefcase on the table, his well-thumbed Bible already in hand. The Bibles he gave out, row up and row down, were pink with blue metallic writing, in an effort to look contemporary and exciting to a class of mixed religion, race and undisputed ignorance. I remember nothing of his teaching apart from the lesson for which he was fired.

This lesson was about a story in the Bible involving rape. Lined up on the desk in a row were four jars with yellow smoky liquid in them. I imagined that it was some sort of dietary special lunch and thought nothing more of it. 'Who knows what rape is?' he asked the class. A swot put up his hand. 'I know, sir. It's forcing the situation.' Mr Chrome smiled. He had a face where all his features except his nose glinted out into a split whenever humour or kindness needed to be expressed.

All through the class he read out the story, touching the individual jars as if to punctuate specific points. A smile would come with a raised head, a moment for us to take note that we had just learned something new. Occasionally he would invite the class to extend its remit to live drama. Slowly getting the point of the story, unease spread through part of the class, transcending the boredom of the rest. The fear of an impending casting session loomed. Gordon, normally from the Tower, was behind me, crushing pencil sharpenings to sell as dope during lunchtime. RE was one subject where no division of intelligence was required.

Mr Chrome asked a few of the girls to come up to the front and look more closely at the jars. There was stuff in them – floating lumps of shell-like flesh. They were foetuses aborted at varying stages of development. The last one must have been about four or five months old, too big for the jar that held it. Nobody said anything as he made a speech about abortion. He didn't explain the word but left his messy delivery of this new knowledge before us. The bell rang and lunchtime arrived. The next week Mr Chrome was gone. A girl had gone home and told her pregnant mother that she knew what the baby inside her looked like. Mr Chrome came back after a while and I saw him through an open classroom door. He never taught us again and RE was replaced with yet another dose of cookery.

Looking back, Sophie and I spotted each other, even when she belonged to somebody else. I had a craving to be near her. In Hampstead you all 'belonged' to somebody or to a bunch of somebodies. Spontaneously, the intelligent buzzed around each other. They were the hippie children – kids of actors, lawyers and writers. They hung around under the giant tree, stretched out on the green at the back, smoking dope undisturbed. Their intelligence and breeding somehow blinded the teaching staff whose job it was to flush out the No.6 smokers from the toilets every lunchtime.

My tendency was to seek out the strong, to befriend those most likely to beat me up. At the age of five, a combination of an August birthday and scarletina, meant I missed out terms of work. On my return, I was rapidly moved up to the class above. Looking back, the yank forward was a crucial year disrupted, affecting my confidence about learning. With no recognizable early talents, I was identified as not that good at much. The social choices were to watch my back continuously, smile a lot and, if not hang around with the fearless, stand as near to them as possible.

The energy in the school changed with the weather. Early summer meant that the house rooms were empty and the school moved outside. Lying close to the hippies and deciding whether to be one of them for that day, I leant back on the grass slope and skewered myself on an HB pencil. A headache of a thud dug between my shoulder blades. I raised myself slightly, grimacing and embarrassed. I asked the girl next to me if she would mind removing the pencil. Giddiness set in as she tugged at it – 'You must sharpen your pencils very well.' The HB snapped off half-way, leaving a good Biba T-shirt shot through and twisted and my back numb. 'They don't put lead in pencils any more – well, not real lead,' said the girl, trying to help. Embarrassment was my main concern, as I swung a cardigan over my back – a strange landscape of tent and wool – and sloped off to the housemaster.

Mr Warmington was in; so was Miss Naylor – rumour had it that Mr Warmington was in Miss Naylor quite often. I knocked on the door.

'Excuse me, sir, I have a pencil in my back.'

'Who stabbed you?' he joked.

'No, I'm serious. I have an HB in my back.'

He came around the desk and asked me to take my T-shirt off, then quickly realized this was not possible as it was pinned to me by the pencil. He asked me to raise it as high as I could while I did a staggered twirl. The odour of Miss Naylor still determining the way this was going, he slowly slid his hands on to my back and shoulders and tugged the pencil out. A piece of lead still lies beneath my skin. He left the room in silence and shut me in. I rearranged myself and came out seconds later, alone – a dirty witness to their affair.

I was one of the ones who, feeling fearful and misplaced, found that it was not the classrooms which terrified, but the corridors in between – the way to and from. Badly lit spaces, they smelt of pencil sharpenings and feet. Packed with bodies swapping places, it was a corridor of murky negotiation, of girl to woman, of boy to man. I remember them as places of gropes and grabs and of reluctant budding and sore flesh. I held my bag to my breasts and tucked my kilt between my legs to form a bizarre pair of shorts, my eyes working hard to scan for possible attack and danger. Regularly spun around, I grew to fear most two who were always before me. I imagined I had no face in these moments, terror tearing off my features. They worked as a team, one taller than the other, both with the same 'shag it if it moves' eyes. It was a speedy and well-rehearsed determination to invade me – in between maths and English, geography and history, and twice a week from biology to PE. They used steel rulers, not for lessons but as part of their battle kit. They were swift. As a pickpocket might bump into you to take your wallet, so they did to me, working their hands in frenzied grabs. With their sharp weapons, they stabbed at the things that marked my gender different from theirs. On the worst occasions they succeeded in pinning my arms back, my bag lost some-where along the corridor. The taller one with black-blue eyes would bend back the ruler and snap it hard on my developing breasts. Disoriented in the crowds, I never fought back. After a while, as the torment on me increased, I went to tell Mr Warmington. I was so shaken by the time I got to my classes that I couldn't concentrate – not so much from the pain, which was bad enough, as from the anticipation that in forty minutes it would happen all over again. Though technically Mr Warmington was the right person to report my problem to, I didn't feel he would be much help, his own sexuality getting in the way of any understanding of what I might be going through. He took the boys' names, put his arm around me and guided me out of the room with a 'not to worry so much' smile of concern. The attacks stopped for a couple of weeks, then recommenced.

There was another boy who kept me on a kind of hit list. His name was Mick Mahoney and he was as obviously misplaced as Sophie and I were. He was a considered and self-conscious mix of James Dean and Robert De Niro, and he hung on to their histories as a way of defining his own. A product of the Tower, he was rarely in school and seems to me now to serve as a model of how to survive in a system incapable of recognizing or galvanizing individual talent. With his dark red leather bomber jacket, Ben Sherman shirt and black and white Prince of Wales checked trousers, there was a smart rottenness about him. A Dodger of our time, on his feet he wore creepers or Doc Martens. To remember him physically is to visualize a boy of stillness and of jerking violence. Leaning against the school gates alone, his moments of disengagement with life were sad to witness. He was often banished from school, on view from the occupied classrooms, and I would gaze down on his solitary figure. A Millwall supporter, Mick's Saturday afternoons were as much about kicking in the heads of opposition supporters as watching the match. A club with a reputation for violence, it was a safe bet that bloody retaliation was going to be frequent.

Mick's charisma encouraged a *Clockwork Orange* following among the other boys. Somehow he made them 'bigger'; he lent them his menace – something they lacked and would probably never have. Several members of the group that went on to become Madness were at the school at this time, and with hindsight now that seems another fairly accurate description of Hampstead Comprehensive.

Mick became a bolshie bodyguard of a friend. Soph and he had attended the same primary school and the bonds formed there have remained strong ever since. 'Duchess' was his summing up of me – the price of living in leafy, middle-class Belsize Park and having a writer as a father. That energy I earlier labelled as anger propelled him into becoming the writer he is today, living not that far from where we went to school all that time ago. Ours was a flamenco relationship – I was never really his girlfriend when he, so quietly, was my boyfriend. He watched over us from a distance. It was a gangster's moll of a love that kept us safer in our last years at school together.

We each left with one O-level, sad proof, in case anyone should ask, that our education had been attempted. However, better than our formal education was our street one. Sophie and I cemented our relationship with the choosing of two brothers to be our prospective 'first men'. We had the silent and watchful blessing of Mick and at a disco held in a Kentish Town church hall we planned our liaisons. The reverend was doing good, keeping us in during those early dark hours which determine the choice between the safe road home and the streets and trouble. A long generation away from us, dressed in his frock, he welcomed us in as 'cool' a way as possible. Swaying from foot to foot to Marvin Gaye's 'Let's Get It On', his pace slowly fizzling out over the more sexual lyrics of the record as it progressed. To the vibes of the Fat Back Band, his mild san-dalled hop tried to encourage those not joining in.

It was the darkness I loved, and the four hours' prep with Greg Edwards's soul tunes on Capital Radio. In bits of Biba, Sacha shoes with our own touches, we were 'simply divine'! We discovered the fifties before the Blitz club and proved to be ahead of Biddy and Eve, Boy George and Marilyn. We found gems in Tesco's (denim bomber jeans), treasures at jumble sales and always took pains to smell gorgeous. We danced together, taking it in turns to feel both male and female. We stopped the floor and people stared. Even then, our pas-sion for fashion was too good too soon.

I chose Eddie and Sophie chose David. They were cute – the same yet differ-ent. We'd got the names the wrong way round and I ended up with David, on and off, for seven years. He was an alarming enough chap for the purposes of aggravating my parents and exciting enough for me.

Nights were spent lurking in front of the giant ventilation shafts of an award-winning block of flats nearby. They were our open-air fireplace, blasting out warming air while we huddled and swigged Cinzano. Saying goodbye was always a very long process – anything up to a full half-hour of hip-crunching, teeth-bashing and silence. (A clumsy time, my head burning with anticipation of what was in his.) When I stayed at Sophie's the two brothers would walk us home. They would be in front, discussing, I imagine, how far each one thought he was going to get in the next ten minutes, while Soph and I lagged behind, just bum-staring. Whose was cuter? Whose jeans hung off them just right? And the shoes. In those lay the answer to how long the relationship would last.

On one occasion in Soph's flats I was occupying the floor just outside her door and she and Eddie the floor directly below. A girl of a girl, she giggled a lot. Invisibly connected, we wanted the same things to happen to us at the same time and a twenty-five-minute session of mauling and tongue-washing ensued. The same telepathy worked between Eddie and Dave as to when each had got as far as he was likely to. That night, Eddie got further. Sophie appeared round the banister with a limp after they had gone. Normally she would bound up the stairs to report her version but tonight was different. She approached in the dark, looking shocked.

'He's . . .' she began.

'He's what?' I asked.

'He's . . .' She half giggled and cried. 'He's come in my turn-up.'

'He's *what*?'

'You know – spunked up into my turn-up.'

The limp was a careful and calculated move not to spill its virile content.

At the time it was both humiliating and hilarious. Holding laughter down in the echo of a space, fumbling for keys, we sneaked into her room, carefully removed the perfectly pressed Oxford bags and put them, as if to rest, in the bottom drawer – jumpers on top. The plan was to clean them when her mum and dad weren't looking. They stayed in the drawer for ages, a symbol of her sexual advancement over me. Jealousy has never been a problem in our relationship!

The mornings after were as important as the nights before. Sophie's dad, Gerry, would 'cater, cater', a role normally played by a mother and, unfairly, appreciated far more when undertaken by a dad. He called me Big Hel. I wasn't, but it suited me. I drank a beer mug of tea every morning and he cooked delicious breakfasts and served them to us in bed. Gerry lived in that flat in a particular chair, with all his equipment around him: the stereo, TV, his books, cigarettes and his wine. He proffered wisdom to us from his soft throne, mostly as we left for an evening. 'Best-looking tarts in London'.

In my closest years with that family I shared him quite equally with Sophie, not as a daughter but as a girl who was accepted. I found something in that flat, a haven to experiment, both a freedom and a restriction well suited to breaking the rules that we had to break. Good times were marked by the move of Soph's bedroom from the front of the flat, overlooking a dark square, to the bright, romantic balcony room at the back overlooking the Heath.

Sunday afternoons saw the transformation of Sophie's bedroom into a photographic studio. White bedsheets were strung up to lamps and door knobs. Two single angle-poises were positioned around the room. Soph was an instinctive photographer, make-up artist, lighting expert, set designer and stylist. Her camera was a birthday present and we only ever used black-and-white film.

A third young woman materialized somewhere between me, the lens and Soph's voice. I was strangely removed and absent. In place of me was what Soph thought she could see – I became a glamorous possibility. From Hollywood and probably long dead, this third girl was never a specific star so much as the aura of an era. We thought we had caught her in her teenage years before she had died so tragically young. Coming out of being her was a sad jump into the shabbier clothes which were mine. Once the make-up was off, I couldn't wait to meet her again. The condition of her – this part of me – was always in Soph's hands; I couldn't attain the beautiful without her.

Visions of our muse and others were all around us. In Soph's drawings she could be a nubile combat Amazon. Through her early and wild creativity lay all the imaginings of the woman I would later re-create for myself. We stayed girls for a long time, in no hurry to get to be like the older women around us.

Our relationship filled the void of not good at much and no ambition to be anything in particular. At times Soph and I were one girl, joined by alternating fear and love for our fathers and a shared sadness for our differing mothers. Our bras were the same style, hers black and mine white; her breasts were large, while mine, held back by ballet, were still aching to grow.

The Heath was the way home. I would leave on Sunday night to go back to Belsize Park, the green space that joined the Lido to the railway bridge, where the balcony would disappear. Another corridor. During one summer we were walking across the grass, past the serious cricketers and their slow-life claps, feeling good and on the way. A black boy walked towards us. I was engrossed with Soph but felt the familiar energy of being stalked without the use of my eyes. He walked past and came back.

'Got the time?' he said.

'No,' we said together.

'Got a fag?'

The word 'fag' was no sooner out of his mouth than he punched my body back into the wire diamonds of the fence. I looked at Soph over his shoulder as his hands and body smeared themselves all over me. She was dancing on the spot, a vision of uncoordinated legs, arms and erratic giggles. My fight back was typical and familiar. The animal left me for a moment and went for Sophie's large breasts. Free from him for a second, this ball of crazed gropes passed back and forth between us. In this late summer assault we were linked forward into a time when we would meet men of a gentler touch. The shuffle of his driven urges over, he ran off down the path, leaving us alone. The pattern of recovery for us was always marked with laughter, neither of us insightful enough at that age to deal with it in any other way. I felt the more molested on this occasion. Prettier? A vulnerability sending out involuntary waves of invitation of which I was completely unaware.

I never shared any of my experiences with my parents and I still don't know why. I took it that life was as it was, that it happened with no questioning needed. I didn't fight back, as I had no instinct to. It didn't occur to me that these things weren't meant to happen. We were fourteen.

Shagarama's was the first big move up to serious clubbing. We were merging effortlessly with the hair and fashion stylists, anything up to ten years older than us. The Kentish Town church club known as Blackfriars became the warm-up arena for the real thing. Shag's didn't get going until midnight. Care of Rory, my first best gay pal of many to come, Sophie's hair was dyed bright green and mine pillar-box red.

Rory was all mouth. Wide open more often than was normal, he mostly imitated a silent scream of feigned horror: head always cocked to one side or back, hands and shoulders curving forwards and up to his face. Slowly the word 'out-rage-ous' would come out, or 'to die for' – an unconscious anticipation of the times ahead. The words slam back into my mind with ferocious sadness whenever I think about Aids.

We agreed to be Rory's aesthetic playthings. He was trained at Vidal Sassoon and practised his art at Flickers in Camden Town, and we saw him as a ticket to better things. Once in Shagarama's, he would instruct me to stand under the red spotlight and Sophie under the green. Our commitment to enduring the wrath of our parents in those days was staggering.

We could afford only one drink each, so we had to make it last. Wrapped in the culture of glamour and gays, we were finally at ease: untampered with physically, adored, our skills at dressing with elegant originality deeply admired.

From Shagarama's we roller-skated home, hanging on to the backs of the first milk vans – a four in the morning chance to reverse our lives, to abandon what was normally done for the freedom of not knowing. Passing a bank in Kentish Town with mirrored windows at the break of dawn, Sophie would scream: 'My hair! Just look at my hair!'

I would follow behind her. 'No, look at *my* hair!'

Protected by the world of nightclubs and underground dressing (heat and drugs), I realize that we hadn't a daylight place for the darker version of ourselves. Reflected back were the beginnings of a process to define myself in sunlight. The parts of me that were scary and inappropriate were looking for a way to leave the teenage years of chaos and experiment. In a couple, we were daring with our creativity, and our instinct for what was to come was always ahead of its time. Not much has changed, except that today Caroline Coates is Sophie and what is at stake is far more public and accountable. Changing our image then required nerve and today the same is true. However, although to have an idea in the adult world can be dangerous, it has rarely stopped me from seeking out the new.

From Shagarama's and Manhattan Transfer we moved ambitiously up to Munkbury's and Donna Summer. Prep time for this started at four in the afternoon on any Friday or Saturday. Sitting either end of a scented bath, conversation kept us going until the water went cold. Smelling good was all part of the process. She did my face and then she did hers – I wasn't good at it and I enjoyed being painted. I loved Sophie's vision of me: she could make me 'gorgeous'. With mugs of tea and mirrors on the floors, we ironed and laid clothes out, and as it got darker outside we layered on our night-time garb, leaving at least one hour for mutual appreciation and last-minute alterations.

There were intermittent dashes to the living-room mirror, which gave Soph's dad a glimpse of our progress. Cooking and listening to Radio 4, he was a man of strong moods; a Dennis Potter of a character. I look back on the swings of them with tearful gladness. He is dead now and I still miss him. Occasionally he would give us that 'you're not going out looking like that' look, followed by the blank expression that quietly came over him as he realized we would anyway. Muttering like Mutley, he would shuffle back into his kitchen to continue cooking.

Years later I would occasionally go back to Belsize Park at weekends. I didn't see him again until the week before he died. He was coming down Heath Street in Hampstead on the opposite side of the road before he saw me. He looked sad, as dads can – trailing a trolley to go to Waitrose, same habits, different street. I crossed over to talk to him; he made some comment about me sounding like Thatcher. We said we would keep in touch, in the way you do when you know it won't happen. An hour later our paths crossed in reverse. Walking more slowly and taking breaks up the hill, he didn't see me at all and I didn't stop. Embarrassment had marked my goodbye to the man who saw me through so many changes and scary places.

Munkbury's was in Jermyn Street. To break into this set you needed to know someone and the only way to know someone was to hang around long enough in their midst, oozing what you had to ooze, in the hope that a big pair of wings would glide in and take you there. They did. They belonged to Prince Izadine. He thought us entertaining and probably saw through our 'get the message' glam statement. On the night he got us in, I was wearing my Margot Hemingway face. We had decided that trying to be too chic through and through would be a giveaway to these experts. We donned Marks & Spencer cardigans and carrier bags, green with gold writing. The flip and casual air of 'we don't need money because we've got so much of it' seemed to work. We were in.

Barely sixteen, we were sitting and dancing among men and women of anything up to sixty. Each time we pretended to be someone different. Prince Izadine of Regent's Park, who, incidentally, looked like Prince, enjoyed the fashion show: a new season every week, shopped for and perfected in between the nights and mornings. His personal bodyguard-cum-lover was called Greek George, shorter than us but wide as all three. In the early morning, heels bleeding from dancing in badly fitting cheap shoes, we breakfasted with the black bomber brigade in the Cavendish across the road. At five we would be driven the way only diplomats dare drive in London, with the bass thumping us off the seats. Arriving back at Soph's, we would dump our night skins on the carpet, leave our make-up on and crash until twelve the next day.

We spent most of our teenage years together, from thirteen till nineteen. Soph was present whenever I first felt, saw or loved. Much of the dynamic remains the same; we are different but know what the other means. I have spent time away from her but still feel protected by our friendship. In her presence I am accepted to an extent that is unique for me. Though our lives have taken separate paths – she is a writer and I am a designer – our relationship continues to grow.

3
Touch

Sue had a gruff voice and a masculine appearance and I was attracted to her by something indefinable. My fateful night with her at the Music Machine in Camden Town started in the early evening. Drinking too much and watching an unmemorable band, boredom took us on to the streets outside. Loitering with no intent, she kicked at a milk bottle, one of a series of twelve lined up like skittles outside a shop. They looked tempting to me too and, picking them up and kicking, we smashed our way through the lot. Watching us unseen was a policeman on the other side of the pavement. As he walked towards us, so engrossed was I in my petty crime, I found I couldn't stop until the last bottle was smashed. Sue and I parted, running off in opposite directions. 'Oi, you there!' was the shout which followed us as Sue legged it into the distance and I down an alley with a brick wall at the end. When he approached me, dancing on the spot like a two-year-old, my instinct was to hit him around the head. I missed his face but hit his hat. Within seconds my arm was twisted up behind my back and I was on my way to the local police station.

Disturbing the Peace, Resisting Arrest, Loitering with Intent, Manhandling a Police Officer, Damage to Public Property: I was put in a cell on my own. Sue, who had been caught shortly after, was strip-searched next door. I stayed in the cell for two hours until, at four in the morning, I was called up to the sergeant's desk. Standing in the foyer was my father. There wasn't anything to say. An acne-ridden officer aged about twenty-five started to lecture my father on how to handle teenagers of my sort. Had my father carried out what was in his head, we would both have been escorted back down to the cells. All charges were dropped. Mr Plod was a fan of *This Sporting Life* and he was sure that this was not my usual behaviour.

Outside, over the bonnet of the car, I told my father that he wouldn't have to do this again. Expecting the bollocking of a lifetime, there was silence. This was the end of a rebellion, as a few days later we sat down to talk about what I should do with my life. Gathering up my doodles and drawings from over the years, he made a portfolio, beautifully framed in dark-coloured card. Watercolour flowers and sketches of Donna Summer got me on to an art foundation course at the only school with a vacancy, Kingston Polytechnic.

My early twenties were the years that changed me for ever, or began me again. Kingston Poly had assembled a workshop of a place in a disused garage to house the course. Entry was through a hatch door with a trip-up section at the bottom. To pass through successfully, a duck and a stride were needed in order not to land on the concrete beyond. A recycled building holding an ad hoc tribe of untamed people: home at last.

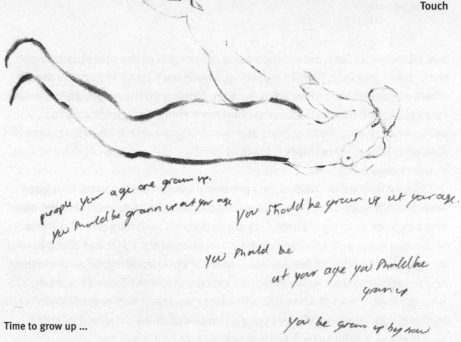

people your age are grown up.

you should be grown up at your age

You should be grown up at your age.

you should be
at your age you should be
grown up

You be grown up by now

Time to grow up ...

Our first day, sizing up the sexes, we were asked to pair off, disappear into Kingston for the afternoon, find something of interest to draw and report back at five o'clock. Much could be learned, I'm sure, by witnessing the first meandering social contacts – who picked whom for the afternoon. I copped out and turned to the out-of-focus body next to mine, a ginger-haired boy with pressed Levi's and a set of well-used Rapidograph pens lying across his lap.

Simon and I wandered into town. This was home turf for him but could have been anywhere to me and my school pencil-case, a sad bag of transitional implements underused and unfamiliar in my hands. Simon liked buildings, Simon liked perspective and shadow and knew all the short-cuts.

It takes years to find out which texture, which point delivers the real you. Borrowing his Rapidographs, I scratched forlornly at the page, waiting until the last minute to find my image. I watched Simon doing his drawings, one after the other, good enough to sell as postcards of the area, and with fifteen minutes left I announced that I wanted to go my own way and would meet him back at the shed. I finally sat on a wall opposite the entrance with the awful realization that I was going to be found out on day one – I had come to art school and I couldn't observe or draw.

Nothing I felt I could draw would sit still for long enough and all that would was past my skills of interpretation. A cat lay asleep in the sun by the doorway and I doodled its form nervously, adding my version of the roof structure and the overhanging tree. Picking myself up, I went back into the fine arts studio, where about eighteen other students were pinning up their work on the walls. I was staggered by what I saw; they had been churning it out in charcoal, paint, wax crayons, Rotring, pens and inks – bright visions, all of them acceptable and convincing to the eye. I tacked mine up in the middle of the end section and awaited the crit.

Slowly it dawned on me that we were being assessed not just for how good or technically skilled we were but for what we had picked up on in the first place and why. I waited in agony until they got to my picture. A long pause at the lack of line and detail and a shifting of shoes and coughs started. I was about to raise an apology when the art teacher said, 'Now, this is interesting. Of all the history and water in Kingston, Helen gives us a cat.' Giggles went around the room. He continued, 'Henri Matisse had a line like this one.' I had vaguely heard of Matisse. With two more students to go, I raced out of the door on the 'Thank you, that's all it is for today,' and downed my first pint in the bar.

The structure of the course was to do a bit of everything until something stuck and defined you closer to where you might end up. In parallel, sexual orientation or the lack of it pinballed its way throughout the year. Straight became bent; unsure became rampant, and the few with no experience had a go at everything with abandon.

I was still looking for my place in the future through those who taught me. Scott seemed like one of us, in disguise as a master of sculpture. He drank most of the day away in the cabin called the staffroom. He romantically labelled himself a sea captain when not attempting to teach our rabble. At the height of rumour, he was a part-time smuggler of drugs, truth and sex. When I wasn't quietly infatuated by his humour and Blade-Runner charm, my love ran towards men who in turn had great loves for others of their own sex.

Tom was Irish and wild, with no pronounced sexual orientation when we first knew each other. He was a rebel, a leprechaun who locked himself into the studio and set fire to his own paintings. Screaming abuse during lunch hours and late at night, he had all the outward signs of a soap-opera artist.

Stephen was Welsh – still is – and at first we were close. He had an incredible (for his age, phenomenal) skill at pattern-cutting and sewing, and we spotted each other as the future stars of the fashion class. There are few subjects other than fashion which so blatantly display the student as beginner. In all the other classes, mistakes, ramblings and unfinished qualities could lead to reason, hope or finality. In fashion, where money intercepts on day one and the number of people who will want it defines a piece's merit, there is nowhere to rest or hide.

I look back at the constraints of the projects and wonder why I didn't slink off sideways into the world of theatrical costumes, for that is all one could really say my primary days in clothes were about. In a naïve place, unchallenged thoughts came to mind of garments cut with no stitches or seams needed, of fabrics whose texture conjured up moods and of knitting which left the wearer as a human maypole. It was the tutors' duty to knock shape and realism into the dreamers and to keep alive the hope that the talents of the people in front of them could come to some sort of creative deal with themselves. It was unusual for students to come to a course like this with making money on their minds and so it was perhaps here that the real-world dilemma of cash versus creativity was tackled early and head on.

There was only one project during the year that allowed me to see for myself how hard and vital things were going to be. The idea was to pick an existing retail outlet and design and price a range for it. My drawings of women at that stage were pretty ET-like and I had no feeling for bodies, just ideas or concepts. Brown's of South Molton Street was always picked, the ultimate in an excuse to design what the hell you liked.

It was during the project that I sensed for the first time from the outside that I had something; something that was mine alone was emerging. I didn't recognize it visually but became aware of it socially as my appearance and personality took flight with its discovery. These were the people I loved being with, the only place to be. The tutors were a dangerous mix of knowing what the real world was like and yet being relaxed about whether any of us might ever end up in it.

The thin garage walls held us in very securely until the day Daphne Brooker came over from the main school to select those she felt had promise. I had been lulled into a dreamscape of permanence, I didn't think it was going to end, but with her arrival fresh air awoke me to a new challenge. I had been in nursery school and the real thing awaited me in Knights Park.

Stephen, Sandy, Nigel and I were selected to be interviewed as prospective candidates for the Knights Park main school on the BA honours fashion degree course. Quite bizarrely, on my interview, I had made myself an outfit which in retrospect had me up for the main part as a bumble bee. In black and yellow-striped towelling, I strode into my interview. I also wore Venetian-blind sunglasses, which quite prophetically shut on the selection panel as they started to speak. Embarrassed, I took them off and carried on displaying my work and selling myself as best I could. A number of weeks later we were told that three out of the four of us had been accepted, and with great sadness we said goodbye to Nigel.

Without doubt, my path towards becoming an eventual designer was set the day I met Richard Nott. A spirit you would imagine could not stay long in one place did, and he saw me through three years of maverick uncertainty. In my younger days in ballet, I would thrust the supple in me into the face of the teacher – a lack of control and wide-eyed exaggeration I thought necessary to mark me out from the rest. Overdoing it was my trademark still years later, as each design had the potential of twenty more dripping off it. Focusing me needed patience.

Richard's gifts remain as strong to this day. No matter what the talent or the presentation of it, he can locate the good, even when the originator is blind to his choices. The most difficult job is packaging the wild and the determined ones, for this is an awkward and at times irrational thing to do. Yet new and unplaced talent I felt I had, as did others, most notably John Richmond, who was two years behind me.

For all Richard's direction, it was Daphne's brick walls that forced inner debate on whether to fight or not. The same questions asked and answered automatically now, were understood by me then as provocative, inappropriate and missing the point: Can you wear it? Can you wash it? Who would want to wear it? And where?

When we were first taught, we had to make our early designs up in spot and cross paper – a necessary cruelty to limit expense and teach us respect for real cloth when finally we cut into it. My love of fabric began when Lycra and I first met in a darkened stockroom. It was cold, slippery and heavy; metres of stuff which went wherever I wanted it to go. From childhood I have associated 'touch' with darkness: twisted tight in heavy curtains for hide-and-seek, rigid cold in cotton sheets tucked under me when ill. The first time I found my mother's wedding dress was in a large, darkened cupboard in the hall; my hands in first, I felt the cut of it, the lace and the net before I ever saw it. I have a way of shutting down my visual response to fabric, as my first reaction has to be tactile. I do this without closing my eyes and it is only for a split second. (This is an approach I may well have benefited from had I also applied it to people in my life!)

I knew the stockroom at Kingston well. I will never forget the day I was accused of stealing fabric. Guilt shot through me, ensuring that the same question was asked of me twice. I was guilty, not of the crime in question, but of misunderstood and fetish-like behaviour that was often displayed when choosing fabric for a project – in the dark. Beyond having character, textiles for me evoke emotions: those that in youth were written foul on walls and in discolouring and chopping my hair. At Kingston, finally, they had a place.

Anyone entering Kingston's BA fashion course considering themselves vaguely an artist either moved up two floors to the fine arts department or was redirected towards the provinces after the first year's probation. Commercially brutal, Daphne was one of the first in authority to run a course with the blood of the real world as a constant reminder of what it means to survive commercially. She was feared, loathed and loved in equal measure and, as in many dynamic relationships of quality, hers and Richard's stormed through to produce some of the greatest design talents in the country.

The most irregular-shaped stone was a young Glenda Bailey, famed for her editorship of British *Marie Claire* and now bringing her influence to bear on the US version. If I was a challenge because of my theatrical approach, then she was perceived as a mountain to climb. As feisty then as she is now, the years of misplacement as a designer only fired her up all the more to build the magazine seemingly single-handed, in the way she wanted it, at odds with traditional expectations of what a fashion magazine editor should be. She made her own rules then, courageously stuck to them and reaps the benefit now.

The day I most understood Richard was marked by the death of John Lennon, whose music had accompanied me through my childhood. My father found much in his lyrics: they reflected back parts of his own life. I was alone in my bedsit when I heard the news, lying in bed. I had switched on the tiny Roberts radio I always had with me and, half awake, heard that he had been shot outside his home in New York and that they could now confirm he was dead. I didn't feel anything until the following Monday, when Richard came into the studio with a black band tied around the sleeve of his white shirt. The optical noise caused silence. He had made it personal and possible to grieve for a great loss in public. I don't think we discussed how it affected us, though, but in his statement I felt less alone and from then on recognized a rare and welcome part of myself in him.

Ron first came into my life as one of three six-footers plus in the architecture department. Regularly persuaded to model for menswear projects, they found the camp and girly atmosphere of the fashion department amusing. We first collided when I zipped the hairs on the inside of his thighs while demonstrating how my men's trousers could also be shorts. Getting good marks, I offered to buy him a Guinness in the bar, compensation for lack of fuss.

By the time Kingston came to an end I had been knocked into as good a shape as was possible. Still living rather in the Land of Nod in terms of what I hoped the average woman would agree to wear, I was a wiser and more considered designer. There had been no projects or awards at college that indicated an instant future in the world of work. After a three-month break windsurfing in Greece, I stopped off on the way home to Rome and by fluke walked into Valentino's on the day a pre-trial version of myself was walking out. I didn't go home.

4

Scent

My interview was brief. The charming Luciano had been a good friend to Kingston Polytechnic and as Richard Nott had also trained at Valentino's years before, the link remained open. As soon as I put foot in the Palazzo, I knew my work was inappropriate and so I was surprised when ten minutes later my portfolio and a smiling Luciano returned to inform a bronzed hippie fresh off the beach from Corfu that I had a job – could I come back next Monday to start? Beyond being enthusiastic, English and vaguely blonde, I will never know what it was that got me the position.

The skills I picked up at both my Italian jobs were useful. The differences between Italian and English women were big in some ways and non-existent in others. I felt for many of the signoras, most but not all safely defined only by the labels at the back of their neck. The pressure on them to look somebody was enormous. This was Rome in October 1981. The perfume changed and, no matter what the weather, the furs came out.

My observations of Italian women were made through the eyes of a twenty-two year-old girl from a background that had seen me through tomboy, skin-head, hippie, punk and glamour queen. On my way to work on the first day, a punk from London was walking ghost-like up Via Condotti. Unaccompanied and uncamouflaged, he had all the heads in the street turn after him in sequence. The carabinieri arrested him and took him away – the charge, I assume, Disturbing the Peace, and inadvertently disturbing mine. Signoraism is peaceful – it disturbs nothing. At that time, it was neat, pressed-bloused and belted. It coordinated a personality away into a uniform of besuited chic. The passion for clothes in Italy starts young, not in the explorative sense as here in England, but as a move towards acceptability. Security and identity are gained *en masse*. Want is less individual; it is a collective and unquestioning passion for fashion, a desire that has long underwritten their industry in a way ours isn't.

In the early eighties to be a rebel or to conform was easy for me either way. The uniform in summer for the young was: white jeans, cotton shirt, soft suede shoes, Raybans and Vespas. The evenings saw many of the young girls dressed as game-show hostesses – a love of colour, glitz, dazzling and cheap. Embroidery played a large part in celebrating the night. Just as grey suits by day do for men in the City, a young signora's dress habits allow the personality of the wearer to take preference. With no individualism or message in the clothes, the face, eyes, voice and energy were the only determining factors discernible to the onlooker. The predictability of it all was sad. In the hurry from signorina to signora there was no rebellion and experiment was non-existent.

At its worst, Signoraism was, and is, a form of snobbery – a lazy attitude to life that said provided the exterior looked tanned, thin and 'hot', then the interior could remain under wraps, unrevealed by the next dress or cocktail party. Self-worth was transcribed into an Armani jacket or a Valentino dress. The beginning of the transition from girl to woman was marked by clothes inspiring confidence, allowing relationships to start and respectability to be confirmed. Certainly the Italians as a nation have an enviable spontaneity with regard to beauty which we lack. Italian women celebrate themselves free of apparent guilt. They have a sunshine ease with their femininity, while we continue to wrestle with ours here.

I tried in vain to adopt the uniform and in the process came to understand something of the habits of a transvestite, only in my case I was unhappy and unconvincing. Living in Rome was how it should have been: equal measures of pleasure and pain. My first place of rest was a *pensione*, just by Stazione Termini, the Italian equivalent of King's Cross. I tried many hotels but, not knowing Rome at all, I nervously stuck close to the station. I had made a bet with an architectural student friend in a bar in Kingston one night – first one to Rome. As far as the initial part of the Italian adventure went, I need not have rushed.

Pensione Alice was romantically dark and dusty, worryingly quiet and picked out of the leftover list I had made on my first afternoon alone. I look back and wonder how I managed to get there. The move was fuelled partly by a broken heart left in London and partly by the realization that England held nothing for me. There were no rooms left in the *pensione,* but misery on my weary face provoked a twinkle of an idea in the proprietor's eye. I followed him stair by stair to the fifth floor and along the corridor which ran around a central, dark well. I looked down on a courtyard filled with palm plants. In the centre was a black-and-white tiled floor – home to a fountain that never worked.

The room was the paraffin storage space. He started moving the orange plastic containers out of the room to reveal a wire-framed bed and a yellow and beige stained mattress. I should have said, 'You've got to be joking,' but, like a lamb to slaughter, I smiled. He was pleased to have solved my problem, and looking at my backpack appearance, no doubt thought it was suitable and miles away from inappropriate. I acknowledged acceptance in English – *gelato*, my only Italian word – and sat in the dark, wondering what the hell I was doing. I spent the first weeks there alone. Danny (my bet from Kingston) finally turned up to share my paraffin paradise in an adjoining room. My nights' sleep were broken and I had to tie a sweatshirt round my thighs to stop old bedsprings piercing them. To Danny, whose male opinion and appraisal I was desperately awaiting, the *pensione* was all part of our adventure. To me, attending interviews at places like Valentino's, it was a polarizing experience. Worried I would carry the fumes with me, I wore powerful and cheap perfume. My clothes I left hanging on wire hangers in the well and I bought an iron – not deemed a necessary expense for an architect! – the smallest iron I have ever seen.

Within my first few hours at Valentino's I was told by the head of studio not to imagine for one moment that I was there in my capacity as a designer, but that I might look good behind the vacant desk in the studio. Naïvely it took me a whole year to realize that this particular woman had a powder habit and was mentally deranged. I learned to sense her and her attacks on the post I had just taken with weekend-long anticipation. Old school skills were stretched to the full, but I still took far too much shit for far too long.

In all the places I have worked where significant success has been achieved around a personality, there have always been the extras. These people keep the aura humming, conducting the singing of praise to the already converted. They exist not for any significant talent of their own, but by association with the genuine article. I couldn't begin to explain to my architect friends what the situation was like. There is a force in fashion, at the very top level, that invents its own manners, sensitivity, standards and rules. They bear no relation to the real world. Untouched by recession, they went challenged. The force is a long way from the beginning. In the eighties the force was success. It lies somewhere between the arrogance it takes to get the creative work done and a gift to match that audacity. It moves itself from the private occupation of designer and blank page to the family-like arena of the company and finally, under a form of glorious madness, to a celebration of it through a fashion show. Once publicly applauded through sales and favourable opinion, the force gains a freedom. It has become a power, still leashed to its owner but now also independent of it. The power can be shared and diversifies its label into other commercial enterprises – most often culminating in perfume. From nothing a long time ago, the indefinable has a value, the intangible becomes a dictator of people's taste.

While at Valentino's I was aware of anything up to forty collections being

designed, not large, elaborate ones but smaller groups dissected into commodities known as licensees. Within each fashion-spending country there is
scope to merchandise a collection to its own needs and, to some extent, tastes.
The brilliance of Valentino as a designer and the marketing of him by Giametti
meant that from *alta moda* one could design Valentino ski, children's wear, eye-
wear, interiors, lingerie, swimwear etc. This is what a designer-made empire
looks like on the inside.

In the main, my job was to work on these licensees, to help translate the
pure V factor into a more available product, income from which could support
and justify the uncompromising vision of Valentino couture. It is this dynamic
that is absent in British fashion. With no public value attached to the perfecting of a craft, there is virtually nothing to commercialize. British money has
never understood how important the dreaming part is.

In way out of my depth, it wasn't a job so much as a further education in
people; specifically those whose lives were devoted to the Valentino woman.
I learned who she was, who she would most like to marry, her taste in music
and literature, the scent of her and the seasonal blessings she craved from
Valentino's hands. Valentino knew who his woman was. While I was there, her
specific nature was an elusive mix of a recalled Jackie Onassis, a Brazilian
model called Dalma and an internal aspiration towards beauty he carried with
him always. It pulled him ahead to each new season. She moved somewhat,
but was never far from perfection. When I observed different women from
around the world coming in for fittings, it always astonished me how, no matter
what their differences, they always came out of the dressing-room looking like
the original sketch. Valentino designed a vision of woman with no individual
specifically in mind, but without fail nearly all of them wanted to be 'her'. His
gift guarantees a following for as long as he chooses to exercise it. In dressing
and designing the feminine so precisely, his creative success is assured for as
long as girls grow up to become women.

My duties while working at Valentino's could be split into two: those I was
given and those I gave myself. The former from passing pins to developing
Valentino's ideas for other products. I also spent much time with Mr Giametti on
the PR and advertising side. What I learned most from Valentino's was largely
unspoken, and its impact was all the more powerful for the lack of words and
direction – watching him fit a dress, for example. The sketch would have been
handed over to the head of that department. As quick as a drug deal, the information was passed and understood. Days later it would appear before us on a
house model, often in toile and occasionally straight into the real cloth.

Valentino would stand up to greet his work, always somehow knowing to sit when toiles arrived. He rose to continue the process that his eyes had started first. An intense concentration then followed, involving a triangle of the hand that passed the pins, the model in front of him and the woman responsible for the interpretation of his work and its alteration. Outside the triangle nothing else existed until, the work over, the garment was quickly removed and sent out and he was on to the next thing. These bursts of exclusive concentration were where his perfection lay. He worked partly from habit, from years of doing it, but this was also his method of keeping the undoubted image he had of what woman meant to him alive. Great models and stars come and go, but to watch Valentino fit a dress in particular is to know that this woman exists above all of them. She is inside him, given modernity by the transient nature of the face of the moment, but in private she exists beyond all of them anyway.

In the main, Valentino related only to a very tight circle of people. As I was a young trainee, it took a long time before he openly acknowledged me. The creative process and shyness do not allow much beyond the essentials of getting a job done. In this regard only, I can claim to be something of a twin.

I remember being constantly chided by the head of the studio in my first weeks. I was told I had better learn fast who the Valentino woman was. In fact, I knew who she was the first day I saw Valentino dress his house model. It wasn't that I didn't know who she was but rather because I did that I was having difficulty. Though I was in awe of Valentino and all that his company stood for, I began to resent its selectiveness. There wasn't a single part of me that was this woman. She was certain; I wasn't. She had money; I had none. She could lavish time and scent on her body; socializing being her work. Lastly, she was always size 8. A form of brutality comes when seeking or designing for a perceived perfect figure, with a blindness to anything above size 10. I was at this time a size 12 and, adoring Italian food, I had trouble even staying at that.

For all my personal difficulties with not being able to join the Valentino woman's gang, years later I caught myself doing exactly the same thing when I designed for women. I have been asked so many times why designers design clothes for stick-thin women. Designer clothes created with a small size in the mind do not work by simply scaling them up. Fashion design is physical autobiography. We as designers design close to the best authority we have: our own bodies. With men designing for women, this raises all sorts of issues. For myself, I start somewhere near me, with an added vision of what the improved version might look like. One might rework the question and ask why there are not more large men and women designing using knowledge of their own bodies.

In the morning, before Valentino's arrival at about eleven, the head of the studio would come in, spraying the latest scent to disinfect the environment and all living creatures in it. She would then faff around – a court jester, pins at the ready, pencils sharpened – looking mean and immaculate. She was a raven-haired machine of praise operating in three languages, a highly paid but nevertheless rented flatterer to the king, an expensive buck-passer. On good days, she was terrifyingly amusing; on bad, a wild muttering jinx of a woman, bolstering her low self-esteem by dumping blame on those below her.

Valentino's workers – his seamstresses, pattern-cutters, fitters and finishers – laboured two floors down in his *palazzo* in the Piazza. Three large rooms with huge tables were permanently occupied by white-coated women. These ladies were of every shape and size, unified only by their code of dress, forever at odds with the clothes they made. They had dedicated their lives to a world they could never be part of. Glamour needs expert fingers to pull it off convincingly: hemming chiffon seemingly without thread and constructing clothes with military precision. These were his laboratories, each captained by a different lady. Of the three, I remember Anna. In charge of coats and tailoring she had a love-hate relationship with the creator. She knew his every scratch. Her mouth was as loud as her own genius and I found her cynicism amusing. On entering the room for fittings, she would utter *'Buon giorno'*. If she dragged out the word, it was a sign she had a masterpiece in tow; if she snapped it out, she was bringing a problem. When her work was perfect, Valentino would wind her up by not commenting on the fact. Theirs was a matador and bull of a relationship, but her anger was always tolerated, because of the length of time she had been there and in silent acknowledgement from the maestro that she truly knew her stuff.

In the late evenings, when all had gone home except the doorman and the cleaners, I occasionally wandered down to the vacated rooms. The industrious hum and private downstairs politics of the day which had filled the sunny rooms were now dead, the chairs pushed school-like under the tables. From the ceiling, strung up like half-finished children, hung the work of tomorrow. White tissue paper made peach by the Roman light wrapped each creation. I walked underneath these hangers, unknown to the women for whom they were made, marvelling at the thread and precision – a boy's deviant look up the skirts of perfection.

Nobody who was anybody came to Rome without dropping in on the House of Valentino, a home from home for the rich and famous. The place was at its most relaxed on the arrival of celebrities. The buzz was a pay-off for the hard work by all the staff, a family confirmation that all was well. The studio was quiet. Valentino's entrances were always pre-empted by a quick trot of Church's shoes down the three marble steps that linked his inner office to the action room. Through the open door, he could be seen sitting quietly sketching by the window. I will always be transfixed by the gaze of the great as where they are is lost for a moment, as thought and implement travel across a white page, until somebody else needs to know about it.

Giametti came in with a step and a smile and Valentino raised his head, concentration and privacy broken. Behind Giametti the besuited calm of a slow, black giant – a lost Muhammad Ali. For a moment he fixed his eyes on me, mistaking my smile for direction. He was quickly turned around towards Valentino, shook hands, sat down on the large sofa and stared. Mr V made conversation. Ali was still a hulk of a man, made more so by the tightness of his suit. He sat with his legs apart and crouched slightly forward, his arms and hands hanging off the ends of his knees. He cupped his fists. Starting conversations in response to his surroundings, he would stop mid-sentence. Gazing was punctuated by smiles, rediscovering the same thought as if for the first time. The house model came in – usually enough to provoke a grunt of consciousness from any heterosexual. Nothing, as she swivelled past him in perfect form. Without the skills of language, no longer able to dance like a butterfly or sting like a bee, he was slowly and awkwardly ignored. He had let them all down. He stayed until the working atmosphere overtook his presence completely. If courage and authority had been on my side, I would have hugged him and sat with him on the sofa as no one else did. I would have told him how my father had thought he was the greatest, and I how I grew up watching him, mimicking his blows in our living-room. In the event, I said nothing and the big man was guided out of the room.

The statuesque naked body of Janice Dickenson stood X-shaped in Valentino's office window. Her butt, at the time Mick Jagger's to touch, shone down to the Piazza di Spagna below. Her taut front was rude and out of place in his office. I was handing some sketches over to Mr V. She paraded her nakedness over antique chairs, flattened her back and crotch against priceless paintings and doodled at God's desk. It was good to see Valentino relaxed, as, half astonished and intoxicated by her he watched as she smudged away all the preciousness, all the luxury and art, with her loud red mouth, free-flying limbs and inhibition.

Prominent in my mind was the visit to the salon by Brooke Shields. Valentino loved her, her youth and beauty mirroring some inside vision of what he hoped always to be able to dress. It was an odd occasion. Brooke, there with her mother, would appear and reappear through swing doors of glass – a photograph away to close-up, with an off-the-planet aura that only the famous exude. Somehow they are images, not flesh and blood, their less beautiful angles edited out. With the protection of projection broken, she was as imperfect as us all. She must have been sixteen or so, and in every move she made she was sad – not to the eye, but to the heart. Her mother plucked the strings; her harp of a daughter could only perform. Even in Valentino's company, where she could have allowed herself some time off, there was none.

'Misha!' Valentino's voice rose with delight, as if welcoming fire. Valentino was at his desk and I lifted my head just in time to see a man leap from a virtual standing position to the desktop. In my mind I had pictured Marisa Berenson and in her place, bird-footed and taut in slacks, stood Mikhail Baryshnikov. Sleeves rolled up and shirt partially undone, he held his arms in fifth position and smiled down at Valentino. I have never seen the qualities of a boy so instantly welcome in a man. 'How's Jessica?' asked Valentino. 'She's fine,' Baryshnikov replied and with that leapt back off the desk. What was natural to him seemed magical to us in the middle of our sketching day. Still beaming from the novel interruption, Valentino led him into his private office.

The business of fashion moves fast. It can hide the still in all of us, never allowing you to be happy with what you've got. Next season . . . It will make it unrequired. The unreal desirable, these are the touch-me, don't-touch-me years when the most money is made. In being ranked close to the bottom of the pile, I could hide behind lack of experience, even stupidity. A jester with no jokes or tricks, I was always around to hear and feel the unsaid.

My hounding by the head of the studio (Mad Woman) persisted on a day-to-day level and at the height of my unhappiness, which had nothing to do with the man himself, I had what amounted to a breakdown. Anyone who knew me could have seen it coming; had I an inkling of what to look for, I could have spotted the signs myself. I ate constantly but was always hungry. I was ashamed at the volume of food I consumed. I would concoct a series of people to meet during a night in order to maintain that I had not already eaten.

I could see I was getting bigger and fought my body with hatred in a place where, had it been perfect, it may in itself have been good enough. Surrounded by males but no love, confronted by beauty in women I perceived as perfect, ostracized for my combat-like qualities amidst the waft of couture, I was lost. Convinced I was being talked about constantly, I became fluent in Italian rapidly. I felt like a hot mistake and began to uncontrollably sabotage any work given to me – surely perverse proof that the whispers were real, I was undeniably bad.

Outwardly, my inner collapse of confidence was marked by a bizarre hair-cut. Hair long and healthy to my lower back was chopped and swapped for a footballer's perm. The constant attention to beauty was suffocating. Any worth I may have had on the inside was glimpsed by Giametti but had nowhere to surface during my stay at Valentino's. Sitting next to me in the top hair salon in Rome, giving calculated directions, was Mad Woman. I sat there, helpless, while years of my identity fell to the floor. I remember smiling all the while and, as the rollers came out of my hair, Mad Woman smiled back at an unfamiliar silhouette and left. Kirby grips and gel became the only path back to someone I vaguely knew.

As is often the case in a place where you tough it or die, my odd appearance and neurotic behaviour went uncommented on. Painfully, camouflage had finally been achieved. I cried in lifts and toilets and finally to the payslip girl, whose bad English inadvertently prompted me to remember who I was for a moment. I carried on throughout this period, only recognizing it for what it was in happier times.

My responsibilities were at their height during shows and the photographic campaigns which ran for three weeks twice a year. My alienation was either saved or prolonged, depending on the duty. For shows in Rome it was Big Hel's job to wake up the supermodels of the day. Tapping hesitantly on hotel doors in the early morning, ignoring the 'Do Not Disturb' signs, my head shrank into my shoulders, as brash American and complicated French accents barked back, telling me what I could go do with myself for the rest of the day. On pain of death, I was told not to come back to headquarters unless I had the famous three either in tow or in the salon, having every treatment it's possible to have. Pedi this, pedi that, manicuring, waxing, brushing, stroking and other masturbatory pleasures these particular superwomen had bestowed on them for their professional hour of glory.

I remember one occasion with fondness, although at the time it was rather alarming: Giametti's request while on a photo shoot. A famous English model of the day needed to be hurried along. 'Send Storey off into the bushes,' was the command. I followed her, without realizing that Mr G had already seen her head that way with a tiny black bag in tow. I imagined it was that time of the month but it wasn't; it was that time of day, and I peered through the hedge to see her frantically shooting up into her foot. Giggles from the other side of the hedge I had come from told me that I had fallen for something again, as I reversed out of the bush to tell them sheepishly what they already knew.

On this particular shoot I did manage to get my own back. I was balancing two reflectors in 100 degrees heat, while the same model was poised six feet up on a plank in a fur coat. In that position she was meant to be aligned to a perfect piece of mosaic backdrop. The inevitable happened when the animal on her back started to smoulder. She complained of the heat – not surprising under the circumstances – and at the last minute, having tilted the reflector only a few times, I shouted 'Fire!' in three languages. Down she came, all six foot of her. My aversion to fur, my fear of drugs and a momentary and rare vision of Giametti losing his cool still provoke a smile. Shortly after, the House of Valentino was among the first to respond to the outcry against wearing fur!

Contrasting with my unhappiness was my love for Rome itself. It has a unique magic: a hazy orange light that struck my eyes from the outset; the food – superbly cooked, never frozen, zapped or reheated; the weight and age of stone and brickwork – sensual; the permanence of the buildings and the light in which they stood – dream-like. Like its people, I eventually took Rome for granted, but in the meantime I became familiar with Rome's language, picking up its equivalent of cockney. The first argument I ever heard, passionate and bloody, was about ham – love, food, weather, clothes and football quickly followed.

The beggars in Rome were a canny lot. The most famous couple were married and worked most of the streets sideways from Via Condotti. He would sit all day long, his body split in half and legless, on a wooden trolley with castors. 'Blind', she would sell flowers on the corner of Via Frattini. As the swallows came down in the evening, he would rise up out of the drain he'd been squatting in all day and she would miraculously rediscover her sight and shut her stall. Never physically arm in arm, they would walk back to Trastevere, where I also lived, a little richer for the day's performance.

I had three homes during my time in Rome. After the paraffin room was Via Pompeii. I had given up the string of three rooms I shared with Danny the architect student when the English 'over there to do nothing much' started abusing our hovel. Wanker John, as he was known, would shuffle his way through most nights. When an English teacher or a nurse accompanied him, his wank to wake the world was replaced by loud Italian exclamations of love – lost on English lasses – and sighs and oh baby's accompanied his rapidly attained satisfaction.

Eighteen months on there were eight ex-Kingston students of the same year from either fashion or architecture. Somehow the more experimental spirit of Kingston had gravitated towards Rome by the early eighties.

Via Pompeii marked the arrival of Ron. He and I shared one room, Martin and Danny had the other two. The boys made a lot of being English. The basement flat was completely tiled shiny green, a swimming-pool of a place to live in, and whenever England played Italy or Argentina they would deliberately leave the french windows open. Provocatively, they would be the only ones for miles around to cheer at any English goals. In contrast to their bravado, I felt socially responsible for our contingent. The only woman of the flat, I smiled at neighbours for all of us in a desperate attempt to defuse the Italians' undecided response to our part in the Falklands War, and to distract them from the boys' loud love of English football. Even so, the hatred was obvious: anything from used condoms to mouldy fruit was dumped on our terrace in retaliation. A response typically Italian, so childlike, it had a sense of humour I miss greatly.

At weekends we would all go off to Ostia, a long beach about forty minutes outside Rome, past Mussolini's monument. One could pick what type of day to have. The beach, marked from one to ten, spanned every type of partnership. In the main, zero to five was for families; between five and eight, was the gay, nude, anything goes – and often did – piece of a beach. We usually stayed at seven, a slightly voyeuristic patch to inhabit.

This beach reflected the span of relationships in Italian life, the faces it wanted to show and the faces it didn't. There was a strong underground life that existed only on the understanding that it wasn't acknowledged. Mother is strong in Italy, even when she's not. Her weight has generations of men striving for power in order to secure her love for infinity. She can never be left. Her boys stay that way – an intimate and childlike arrangement that, despite the

Sketch of Ostia by Ron

years in between, finds itself running a country and organizing power.

My response to Italians has always been emotional; in that, we are compatible. Much of my time was spent with a mix of American painters, British visitors who came to stay and couldn't leave and Italians who sought the company and minds of anyone not Italian. They live a wonderful life, as multilayered and deviant as ours, but held together magically by buildings that will never be built again. The sun liberates an uncomplicated people to enact most of life's emotions in the open air.

I was at my happiest living in an attic in Trastevere. It had two rooms and a stand-up shower. The bedroom/sitting-room, with cracked white plaster walls and marble floor, had a bed which filled the space. Wall-to-wall shuttered windows opened out on to a stage of dusky terracotta rooftops, aerials, trees, a hill and the ever present swallows. The three families in the courtyard below had been arguing together since the beginning of time. They never looked up – our window was known for a transition of faces that wouldn't stay long – so Coppelia-like I looked down upon their shouts and screams, the soundtrack to our year there.

On sunny evenings I would ride home on my bike past the most magnificent architecture in the world, through wafts of coffee and basil and across piazzas of slow drinkers. I would hang on to the back of Vespas, as strangers sped me over the bridges and let me go at the Vatican. Getting home always involved backtracking. Towards the end I was a familiar sight on my bike. Surprisingly few Italians used pushbikes, a Vespa being the universal sign of having attained freedom ticket number one. To be considered vaguely as a local was an accomplishment in this village of a city. Although I had learned the language from fear of being talked about behind my back, the speed with which I picked it up informed me for the first time what it felt like to consciously learn. I could respond to people in Italian in a way I have never been able to in English. As a foreigner I was freed.

My stay at Valentino's could not have lasted much longer. I deeply admired him and learned more from Giametti than ten years in business could do. Together, they set a standard, a level of professionalism, that would remain a benchmark for all my career years to come. At Valentino's I had learned huge amounts: I had seen how a fashion empire can spread confidence and an addiction to being a certain type of woman, and how 'image' in the eighties could convince us
to doubt the most basic things about ourselves. It fascinated me. I never felt male or female there but, invisibly, a middle sex with an exhausting appetite to understand both, and when I left, I felt I did. Though I hadn't been persuaded by the Valentino formula, I did leave with a love of Valentino's glamour – a direction destined to go elsewhere.

The pattern of being set upon by Mad Woman persisted and the humiliation became intolerable. I handed in my notice. It was a day of defeat for me. Five minutes later she came skipping and striding towards me, her long legs gathering speed to impart something important. She made an attempt to pick me up, a heave of an insult by now

The dreaded puffball designed at Lancetti

familiar. 'We've done it,' she whispered. 'Done what?' I replied. Valentino's scent engulfed us both as she said, 'I've handed mine in too.' I stood still, speechless, smothered in the rattle and hush of her cashmere body. In the end, everything about her was soft. Had my world been captured on celluloid, her torment of me would have been rewarded by my pushing her out of the studio window, her chic skinny body splattered on the cobbles of Piazza di Spagna below. In reality I left to work with Lancetti and she went to America to edit a famous magazine.

I saw her years later in New York when I first started to show there. I heard the voice first, chastising a lower somebody, in public. She didn't see me but I saw the face of the young girl on the receiving end. Beamed back five years, I tried to kiss her with my eyes and moved on.

It was Lancetti who benefited from my education at his main competitor's salon. Lancetti was often, and still is, considered very much second best to Valentino. The family at Pino Lancetti's was intimate – welcoming in a way only a smaller company can afford to be. He is the Zandra Rhodes of Italy. His instinct for print makes him closer to a painter than a designer. His insecurities around shape and form lock him into his heyday, the seventies. His customer is not so much international as local, with strong support from the Japanese.

That meant little to me. I simply adored him. He was the moodiest bugger I had ever met, had a liking for wicked water and gave

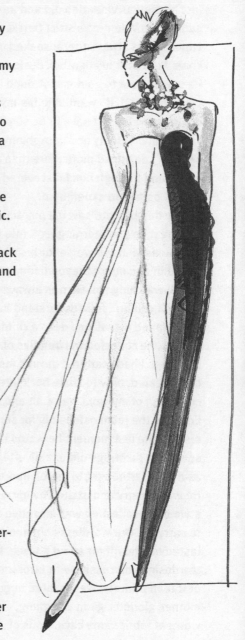

Lancetti's work

me more confidence than I could have wished
for. You could read him by his eyes, always
shining as they gazed out from a greying
beard and flopping grey hair. He didn't project himself as Valentino did and in sharp
contrast to Valentino's strict timekeeping,
Lancetti was always there; soaked into his
chair, bent over his lightbox desk, some days
he seemed not to go home. Around him I
could be a slob if I wanted to be: my hair
could grow; I didn't have to be someone else,
I was sufficient. My eating problems disappeared. I designed more there than ever
since, and through him I discovered my own
love of paint and experiment.

One day Lancetti saw me painting paper,
ripping it up and rearranging it into torn flowers. Somewhat the worse for his whisky, he
paced in and out of the room four or five
times, watching me. He was always convinced I couldn't fully understand Italian. He
encouraged me, as one does a child, twice. In
silence, he collected the bundles of baby
paintings I had scattered around me and
disappeared, only to come back later. His
collection of my work was a hit and run affair.
Entering the room ostensibly for something
else, at the last moment he would cleanly
swipe the paintings under a diverted gaze,
as if an afterthought to more important work.
He was hungry and excited by my work. The
style of its collection was incentive enough
to carry on. Our wordless communication
lasted on and off for about a week. I saw
the designs discussed with Etro, the God
of Italian printers. Weeks later, huge,
mother, glorious, giant, shagging,
wows of fabric came back. Rolls of

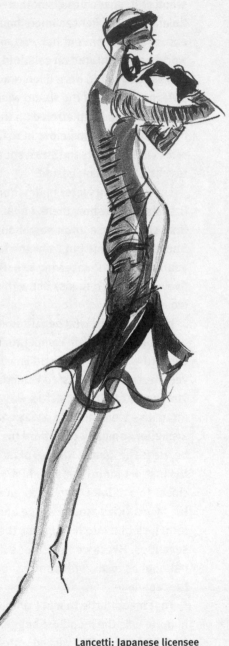

Lancetti: Japanese licensee

them. I could paint; they had worked. Lancetti knew and I loved him for it.

I could have stayed there for all the wrong reasons, except for the day when walking past Alexander's on the corner of the Via Frattini, I was halted by a window dedicated to Bodymap. (Alexander's was a rare shop in this village of chic, one of the first to bring innovation and fast-change ideas to Rome.) I stared at that window, remembering something that I had long lost and hidden away. It was dressed with a black-and-white optical outfit, wildly layered in its proportions. The tailored Signora-ism which had masked me for nearly two years fell away. I knew that the jagged part of me could never make peace with 'her' and I looked for a way to go home.

Ron had been out with me for his year of industrial experience. The design world in Rome sits very much pocket to pocket and so getting a job via the Valentino route was not hard – a strange experience for Ron, as he was in far greater demand from men than from women. He came home blue one day, having had the boss's enormous and wet tongue licking his ear for most of the afternoon. They had been deciding on what shade of pistachio green an Arab customer's swimming-pool house should be. On some level he was quietly flattered that men were open with their delight at his physique.

With the spontaneity of Bodymap's first collection still rattling my cage, and Ron back in London to finish part two of his course, I finally plucked up the courage to tell Lancetti I wanted to leave. We were both upset but didn't show it. He ignored me for a while, transferring his attention to his two other designers, but I sat it out. When it became clear that I wouldn't be changing my mind over money or perks, we parted with much love and the biggest and best book of Erté.

5

Taffeta

Slinky woman for David Sassoon, 1986

The first collection I put together was while I
was working at Bellville Sassoon but designing my own range on the floor at home.
Three years in Italy had passed at Lancetti
and Valentino and I was back in London – an
unimaginably welcome return to Twiglets,
real curry and rain.

A bride to be, 1986

In 1984, London's established names were
Wendy Dagworthy, Betty Jackson, Jasper
Conran and Katherine Hamnett. During
London Fashion weeks, over and above these
names, all three floors of Olympia were
packed solid with designers. From Leigh
Bowery and Rachel Auburn to Stephanie
Cooper and Christine Arherns, it seemed that
anyone who could floor the pedal of a sewing
machine was jumping into the party that was
London. The black-and-white flag that had
been in the window of Alexander's in Rome
was the tip of the iceberg.

Unclear about how to fit my recent experience and my reason for leaving Italy together,
I looked for a job that would make use
of my 'understanding the lady' skills.
Bellville Sassoon, and moreover
David Sassoon, took me on,
my hand having improved
during the time spent
at Lancetti and my
increased respon-
sibility. In a small room
off the shop in Knightsbridge
we designed collections
together. I learned the
language of those
who lunch, race and
ball; how taffeta
does its job so well

when ruched to any waist; and how glamour for most English women was not familiar territory.

English women at this level celebrated flesh very badly – something of a shock after the wriggle and keenness of the Italians. There was then (and things have changed) an ambivalence about parting with money for the physical improvement of themselves. A male consciousness drove both the cost and also a constraint over their sexuality. Many of these women's husbands needed them to look good – but safely. The aim was not so much to have a trophy wife as a woman good and true who would stand by you, smart and inoffensive, intelligent and companionable. There were, of course, the exceptions. These women were notable for their abundance of flesh; not a chance of wearing a corset, so a hat that would turn heads. Bias-cut was anathema to them. Instead, they chose miles of floating chiffon, becoming visions of pink and yellow, loud in voice, laughter and colour. Free from the disciplines which would have produced the desirable thin figure, they enjoyed life's pleasures, dietless and bulging with energy. My favourite lady was Mrs Beckwith-Smith. In a slow flurry, her entrance was as large as she was. From the country and 'up for the day', she would tease the designer about what she might be able to squeeze into this season, before extracting from her basket fresh flowers or herbs for the staff.

The Royals form an important part of any British couturier's clientele. Bellville Sassoon was no exception, and his great kindness, manners and dedication to dressing their individual needs were practised over many years. The Italians have always wanted to get their hands on our Royals. What Valentino could have done for Diana was an often dreamed-about sketch and conversation. A certain lady with a penchant for yellow came often to the shop. She liked the way I drew and painted – I was amazed by my instinctive ability to sketch the look she wanted. I learned all the areas that must or must not show – an intimate experience of witnessing another woman's photographically recorded vision of herself.

Whisked to somewhere quiet and private, ma'am would be made comfortable and sketches, fashion and tea would be served. 'Where's Helen?' she would occasionally ask, and with pad and pen to hand I would bob before her, ready to translate her vision to finished design. We invariably ended up in the place we started, but it didn't matter – I enjoyed the journey. On our yellow afternoon a hemline was in discussion (occasionally what *Vogue* said came into play) and a rehearsal was needed. A lady like this knows every photographic opportunity: when it will be snapped, her angles, her tilt towards light or not,

Two rooms in
Bloomsbury,
1959. My mother,
father & me

When Sophe and I were
one and the same

Jake, Kate, Magda, Becky & me,
1964: 'The Lyndhurst Gang'

Me in my
Biba days, 1972
by Sheila Oliner

From Hollywood and probably
long dead. Sophe's vision
of me, 1974

Rage, as seen in *Elle*

Sequins

Bullet & rose bra

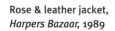

Rose & leather jacket,
Harpers Bazaar, 1989

Abstract Woman

Stella Tennant spits, photographed by Miles Aldridge

Barbarian
Woman

Primitive Instincts

Diamonds Fall

Second Skins

Opposite page:
Sandra Bernhard for *Vogue*,
1994, by Sante D'Orazio

Pomp & Circumstance

Kingfisher

Second-hand Rose.
Multi-shirt ball skirt, *Elle*, 1992

Tea for One suit

Freida

Madhatter's suit

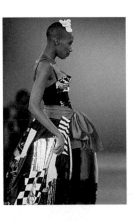

Rich Rubbish ballgown
from collections' scraps

Paprika silk, 1994

Providence. Neil Kirk for *Vogue,* 1994

Council binliner ballskirt
designed in 1991.
Photographed by
Platon/Hamilton's
Photographers Ltd

the risk of wind or rain, the extent to which flesh may or may not be seen. To my amazement, a line-up of three chairs was assembled and I was called down to help. In the middle chair, facing the back of the one in front, sat ma'am; in the front, the driver (David), hands almost on an imaginary wheel; and the vacant chair at the back was left to give a sensation of vehicle length.

'Helen, you are to open the door,' she said, which of course I did. I tugged down at the imaginary handle and swept it open. Out came the side-cocked ankle (always the first camera shot). Until recently, the picture would have displayed round, tubby-fronted shoes.

'What can you see?' I was asked.

'See, ma'am?'

'What can you see?'

I ducked down to a level I felt beckoned towards.

'Can you see anything as I do *this*?'

'No, ma'am.'

'Good.'

The car was dismantled, the tea finished, the dress off and on to the next appointment into the real thing with wheels. I went back upstairs, bewildered and giggling. Chatting to one of the seamstresses in a break, I asked what all that was about. She whispered in my ear, 'Fanny check.'

On another occasion I sat drawing at my table. I was comfortable at David's and challenged by the constraint of frump that sometimes dictated our brief. I felt an itch at my feet but, alone in the room, couldn't place the irritation. It persisted and swayed my line off. I bent down, my cheek squashed on the table-top, my arm reaching to scratch. My hand came across another one, of a much softer texture. Fingers were rippling, childlike, on the arch of my foot. I jumped back and met Yellow Ma'am's soft, powdered face on the opposite side of the desk – a dismembered yet happy vision. 'Hello, Helen,' she said cheerfully. My reaction must have been worth seeing. No one believed me when I recounted the incident at teatime.

The Royals may have been responsible for teaching me consideration of women, which I am often accused of ignoring. Each woman has her own agenda, moments when she wants to be wild, moments when she has to be solemn and serious. We took every perceived imperfection into account, we cut high or low around the beautiful. The clothes we designed were the perfect foil to their most exquisite gems – history in boxes, rightly milked from generation to generation as adornments to beauty. I observed the Royals not as an institution but as women whom I met in intimate situations. I was never interested in seeing or being at the occasion for which the frock had been intended; my passion was designing an accurate vision of how they wanted to be. I did not judge it, but was drawn into the process of feeling my way around their minds. I was drawn to their eccentric side; theirs was a club for which neither birth nor money were the credentials.

At ease with David, ours was one of those rare relationships of mutual respect. He knew his market, his ladies, and stuck to it. At the same time he had the gift to spot talents very different from his own. For me, progressing from Valentino to Lancetti and finally to Bellville Sassoon was giving me a clearer picture of what I was not.

6

Moves

It was once suggested to me that I designed for women as a homosexual male would. The person saying this was intelligent and knew my work well. Through the years the words have stuck and are worth considering. Do gay men 'do' women better? It might be a generalization, but for me it is true.

The first time I asked myself this question was while observing Valentino with one of his muses in the early eighties. In the run-up to each collection, fittings of the slimmest and most beautiful women in the world took place in his studio. The walls were people-thick: fitters, white-coated assistants, jewellers, milliners, prompters of praise and the general gang that it takes to make pencil line perfect, the real thing. Wearing only a smile and a flesh G-string, they would stalk gracefully into the middle of the room. Mad Woman would check for odour and, if in any doubt, offer a squirt of the latest scent. Once this test had been passed, they would approach the large mirror, in front of which sat Valentino. I could bear to watch only the most competent ones, as their relaxed air was all that helped us hold on to ours.

This particular model knew Valentino well, her body having passed examination, her stride having been blessed, seasons before. And as she stood before him, the mechanics of the process came home to me. Her breasts were not breasts; the G-string's job was to make smooth and mask the feminine sex – of no interest to him; she had young boy's hips and her skin had that perfect tension caught only in the few years between childhood and adolescence.

These boy-women, devoid of genitalia, come before the maestro offering a deal: I can be who you want me to be; I can convince others that you are right. Their job is to be a blank canvas, to become the designer's vision. This scene was not personal to Valentino; rather, it stands as a reference in my mind to a larger discussion. I watched where his eyes stopped, seeing what mattered to him, and questions shot through my head. What, in the process of homosexual male design for women, is avoided in order to cherish them, as they clearly are. The accuracy of the desired vision is on one level ironic, as women have been consciously rejected. The creator will, for instance, never be able to empathize with the conclusion of his successful feminizing of these women. He cannot imagine the night of the pick-up, or ensuing seduction. Where the feminine side of man is strong, though, there is a unique and indescribable ability to objectify what a woman wants. 'Couture sex' takes place. Slightly unreal, detached from the everyday world, a perfectly disconnected love passes between designer and wearer, in truth dressing them both at the same time; a shared passion that diverges only on the trail of sexual fulfilment.

One could argue that women designing for women have no need to feminize blatantly, for they are already there. For them, though, it comes from a genetic authority which can permit the subtle and sexual to take place. There are, of course, exceptions, but even so these do not alter the main drift of the argument. For example, Vivienne Westwood, though well imitated by other greats, can parody women in a way that a male couldn't. Her soul and feminine spirit inform her so totally that what we see could only have come from a woman.

The implication behind the suggestion that I myself design in this idealized and objectified way is that I set women up, that in designing the provocative I ignore the intelligence, that in using clothes as a metaphor I disregard the body and its need for comfort. In reply, I would say that I am never so deliberate, as at the onset it is instinct that informs my work over reason. Any point of view or message that the work may have is often created and read into by others after the event. Certainly each collection does say something of who I am, where I stand in my years and hopefully of my time, but I remain impulsive as to the paths that I follow.

The crime I appear to commit is that being a woman designing for my own sex, I take no responsibility for what I offer women to wear, whether it be leather, plastic or Lycra. However, there is a big but: some of them love it. When you are in the best of my work, you are in the world's 'face', you are at your most vital and, if you want to, you can celebrate all that is both feminine and sexual. If I objectify, it is towards a hope I have for myself; if I am tempted to idealize, it is because perhaps uniquely in my little world I have a healthy fight of male and female within me.

It could be argued that I am jealous or torn, my creative years having been given over in part to my life-child as opposed to my life-work. But I am drawn to satisfy and explore both. The energy that could have been used exclusively for leaving my mark through my work is channelled equally into care and love of my son. In the early days I was always aware of the lack of women with children around me, whether in PR, marketing, modelling, finance or make-up. The pursuit of self was not the result of youth but an unexpressed fear that anything else might be a distraction. Children and the instinct in most women to have them were perceived as split loyalty and as such quietly restricted expectations of how far a woman might go. In my design career you see the snatched, the last-minute, the acute focus that only time running out can bring. Because of all the other parts a designer has to play, along with keeping an eye on the nursery school clock, it was always the actual design work that went to the back of my queue. But since it could be done alone, late at night or on a bus, here was the challenge. Running a design business as a working mother is both a problem and a great focuser of the mind.

The preoccupation with youth in fashion is at odds with those who can afford to buy it. But where is the sexuality in age and wrinkles? Why struggle to portray the average figure as opposed to the slim-line version so easy and pleasing on the eye? As a female designer, designing for women, I too create clothes that do not favour my changing figure. I am as involved with projecting on to women as others are. At its best, though, my strength has been to feel change before it is openly acknowledged.

I asked my son, aged ten, why Pamela Anderson and not Dawn French? His answer: 'Dawn French wobbles *all* over.' And he twisted his mouth and gave a shiver. In truth, I have waited too long to get an objective reply that might help me clarify my thoughts. Television and early signs of puberty have already informed Luke's choices. To me, the shape of Pamela Anderson's body is absurd precisely because it does wobble in only one place. So when does flesh, taut or flabby, become too much? And for whom? Do women want to escape it or do men? Is flesh suffocation and leaness freedom? Is the odour of one bad and the other fragrant?

Some of the answers may lie in the women we have held up as 'super': the best of their kind. The power of these women began to flourish when the 'designers' collective' vision was floundering. A collection's *pièce de résistance* was often made famous more by who wore it than by any genuine strength in the design itself. Though this breed is also now going through change, that supermodels came to exist at all is important for how women view women. Supermodels are the 'impossible women', and the fact that we may aim in youth to be like them sharpens our focus as we grow up on what we ourselves are as women – how much we think looks and size matter, and to whom.

To think that women find the acceptable face of their physicality exclusively in men is perhaps to ignore what women do to women. I have often wondered about my mixed feelings of envy, admiration and quiet relief when watching the supermodels strut their stuff. Does the distraction of their beauty and projected confidence allow us to rest for a moment from performing the very job that they do in front of us: attracting a response from the opposite sex? In watching these women we are seeing the unreal fodder of men's desire, and as a result avoid femininity itself in as much as it is a male-endorsed vision rather than a female one. Even in the state of partnership or marriage we are afforded little time off. We are perpetually courting (consciously or not) the possibility of another man in our lives – one beyond, whether in the shape of an absent father or simply a better deal.

I have come to think that it is not necessarily the image of the supermodel that generates envy on the part of 'normal' women, but that this collected breed stands as a wearisome reminder of how much of our female energy is preoccupied with this dance. It is hard to know nowadays whom the projection of very thin women is ultimately for, given that the visual representation of our sex is seldom balanced by a more voluptuous form. Men claim they prefer a more curvaceous shape – Cindy rather than Kate – and the vast majority of women don't aspire to being skinny anyway. Supermodels have become an extension of 'celebritydom' and, in this sense, emaciation or a size 8 figure is less important than that star quality that must be exuded and perpetuated in order to maintain their status.

The fact that supermodels are primarily silent objects is important. Undistracted by their words – wise, vital or dull – we can play with what it is we like or dislike about the glamorization of our gender. As a designer, how-ever, it is impossible to ignore the magic that surrounds them. And although we must acknowledge that what we are applauding is unachievable in our-selves, there is a luxury in watching a young and beautiful girl with her wis-dom years yet to come; a one-off chance to witness an elegant 'fuck-the-world' attitude so intoxicating when met with a genuine talent for performance (the young Pat Cleveland). After all, how many professions are there in which a girl's looks do not undermine her chances, where her gift can fulfil its purpose instead of serving as a distraction to being taken seriously?

If this boy/woman is really a part of the male homosexual designer's instinctive projection of himself on to women, then we have a third and very powerful vision of Woman. At heart, she is neither male- nor female-inspired but an extraordinary fusion of the best in both; this is worthy of continued celebration and clearly works commercially.

This largely unspoken yet well-known observation carries a mild but unwarranted taboo and has led to endless column inches on the seemingly unfathomable use of skinny models. There is nothing wrong with the naturally thin or the curvaceous, we simply need to find a way to redress the balance. Above all, we must remember the next time we become agitated by the vision of a minority figure that it has never been in the interests of either the fashion or the beauty industry to represent the common form in us all. To do so would, quite simply, stop the machine. At a time when the persistent dilemma of the commercial world is to sell us something we don't necessarily need, it is clear that fashion, rightly or wrongly, currently succeeds only when it carries with it an element of the unattainable.

As youth starts to leave us and skin to pull away from slackened muscles, we must find in ourselves a replacement for the impact our tauter versions occasioned. It is not for nothing that the fashion industry has a vested interest in promoting youth over age. There is little money to be made from women who know exactly what they want. True fashion takes advantage of the space in between – not knowing what we want and searching for the woman we wish to be. Recently, I became obsessed by the quest for a particular camel coat. Having lost my job, buying the Helmut Lang original was not an option. This coat got a mention in every call to my girlfriends and soon they were searching for it as passionately as I was. I was even bought one blind in the hope that it fitted the bill – it didn't. The camel coat, not dissimilar in feel to one my mother had when I was very young, was to mark a change in me. I had to have it. It was a way of confirming an altered part of myself I thought would last.

Clothes mark the changes in women, even for those not as impassioned by them as I am, and if women on the whole feel defined by someone else, then it is not surprising that the fashion world makes more money from them than it does from men. If clothes are sold to us within the supermodel image, then 'real' people must be used as a marketing tool to break down the fantasy that in buying these clothes you too can look like the model. Using real women openly acknowledges that we may not know who woman is at the moment. We can recognize female youth because of its transitory nature and on it we can project almost anything. But the diverse imagery of real women is the only solution. In making her unspecific, we do not have to identify her. The new supermodel could be anyone correctly styled. If she is anyone, then why not thin, fat, young or mature?

7
Beginnings

When I first met Caroline Coates she was sitting in a small upstairs room behind a metal
desk in the West End of London. I remember
blonde hair, the colour purple and a conversation taking place on the phone; the person
on the other end no doubt squirming under
her powers of persuasion. She put the phone
down, another no turned into a yes, and
looked me straight in the eyes.

Parachute dress in ribbed
sea-island cotton, 1986

My Diaghilev was a young woman from
Yorkshire. She has maintained her northern
ticket more successfully than I – a straight-
forwardness, an honesty that is complicated
in the name of sophistication by some
southerners. From the onset, she set about
creating opportunities to build fashion
design companies, this in a country where
the textile trade rarely took any notice of us
designers, to get a collection manufactured
required enormous luck coupled with day and
night persuasion; and there was a fundamental disbelief that design in the hands
of the creative could make money.

Set up in 1982, Amalgamated
Talent was an effort to harness
and capitalize on the talent
pouring out of our art
schools and colleges.
The idea was to coach
students who wanted
to set up on their
own about business,
costings, cash flows,
banks, exporting, insurance,
editing, manufacturing and
finance. In her day, Caroline held the hands
of anything up to eighty designers, equipping
them with the skills that have seen the best

of them come through to leading positions in some of the world's largest firms – Coates Viyella, Calvin Klein and Marks & Spencer.

Starting out on my own had been little more than a reaction to dressing women with whom I had nothing in common. The vision for the label was still located in glamour but was to be found somewhere between Bruce Oldfield's early work in the eighties and the high street. It was an unconscious mix of me and Biba with edge. From the beginning, my belief in myself was fuelled by a need to find out what kind of designer I really was. I had no idea what was in store for me, which was not so much naïvety as following the part of my character that was prepared to risk, and, perhaps as importantly, had an energy to match. This was the moment which demonstrated the future dynamic of our partnership. Who planted the first thought was to be characteristically unclear: a thrown look, an over the shoulder courtship, demonstrated through what she was already doing for others; from me, an invitation to be coerced. Somewhere in her I unconsciously located the strengths of both my mother and my father, at once nurturing and persuasive. The trust which rapidly built up between us, combined with a practical need for partnership, gently convinced me I was in the right place.

At the time of designing my first collection, I was still working with David at Bellville Sassoon, making mad dashes between his world of taffeta and my other life in denim. Despite my accuracy at fulfilling the brief for the county ladies, I had a rougher, more experimental side. Denim was miles away from chiffon and I was drawn to a cloth

1/2 + 1/2 dress, 1986

that I could beat up, bleach or rip. After first
meeting Caroline, she had got me together
with Wrangler to do a range that considered
the roundness of women and my first collection for Spring/Summer 1986 was a continu-
ation of this.

'Distort' shirt and
skirt-cum-shorts, all in
sea-island cotton, 1986

Through an inability to get at the heavy-
duty machinery which gives denim its authen-
ticity, I decided to take it in the opposite
direction and produce denim which was feminine. I designed jeans that fitted into the
waist and hung just right, low on the hips,
using denim's selvages and fraying qualities
to the full. Shift dresses and jeans con-
structed inside-out had Macey's of New York
buying my *Pompidou Centre* collection for the
first time. The only other cloths were a white
sea-island cotton and orange cotton Lycra. In
the vests and T-shirts I inserted elastic pan-
elling below the breast to give an early suggestion of 'pleased to see me nonsense' at the
front. A young unheard-of Naomi Campbell
walked my first dress in one of her first
shows. The *Pompidou Centre* collection produced just five orders,
but it was enough of a taste
to hurl me forward towards
the next collection.

When seasons
were still seasons,
and the words
'diffusion', 'trans-
ition', 'holiday' and
'cruise' hadn't yet hit
home, it was always a
renewing experience to
jump from summer to winter.
Oil was my second collection, and

the first to be sponsored. Although the range, apart from its coloration, had only a flimsy connection to the sponsor, what BP saw was an entrepreneurial spirit and a concept of design they liked enough to back. As far as we knew, this was the first sponsorship agreement between a non-clothing company and a fashion designer.

Again, I limited myself to a few fabrics – in part because financially I had no choice, but also because, in a range of less than twenty styles, any more would have made the collection incoherent. My first foray into handknits for *Oil* took me to deepest Clerkenwell and a dizzy broad fraught with problems. To build up any label in fashion design is as much about taking on the world of people as it is about design itself. Developing a team who have expertise and can be trusted is essential to growth. The ability to cajole, flatter and bully is as vital as any flair for picking the right silhouette or the perfect button. At this stage in my early career I was a two-woman band – Caroline and myself.

Once on the roll of the next collection, you are sucked into the day-to-day and the short-term with an equal measure of excitement and dread. As each new collection takes shape on paper, a form of courage is required to not always take the route that is obvious or close to hand. Among my mistakes, however, perhaps one of the biggest has been not standing still long enough to make the most of a risk. No sooner has one idea got out and been made up than there is an inner surge to replace it. It is only when a young company has grown to the stage where it can get to its market-place effectively that ideas-led designers can make their mark and, for that matter, their money.

In our early days, it was – and still is – the British Knitting Clothing Export Council (BKCEC) that best identified and supported the possibility of exporting and exhibiting abroad. In 1987 I designed a collection for Spring/Summer called *Industrial Rose,* sponsored by YKK Zips UK Ltd. It was on one such trip to a New York show that marketing and design came together for the first time. By turning zips into the petal definition of roses, I had started my journey of challenging the expected use of trims and cloth. Very slowly, under the umbrella of Amalgamated Talent, and still one of twelve other designers, I was carving out a niche for myself. Early on I realized that it was only by offering something different that I might find a place for myself long-term. Around this third collection the Japanese buyers hovered, the Americans bought and the Italians fell in love. I had my first window in Alexander's of Rome.

Autumn/Winter 1987 was my fourth collection, titled *Nijinsky*. It was here that I first began to understand the importance of theme, not only for myself – as a way of keeping a wandering mind specific – but also as a method of selling a collection to buyers and, ultimately, the consumer. *Nijinsky* harked back to one of my greatest influences. While at Kingston I had read his diaries, edited by his sister. They depicted the decline of his sanity against a parallel growth in his genius as a dancer. In the diaries I saw a struggle and a talent to which I was drawn. With a sane jealousy, I longed for a time when the worlds of music, art, fashion and dance could somehow clash or kiss. Stravinsky, Diaghilev, Picasso, Chanel and Nijinsky had all worked together at one stage and if ever a time like that could reoccur, I fantasized England was the place for it.

The ballet, *L'Après-midi d'un Faune*, gave the collection its black and white dictation and, apart from the prints, it was the detail which marked it out as special. I designed hosiery for the first time: Nijinsky sat crouched around the ankle in perfect poise. When worn, he stretched and twisted to the thigh, as if in a slow-motion leap up the leg of the wearer. The collection took me into many more American stores and a long relationship with the USA started. *Nijinsky* was bought by Saks, Fifth Avenue, Henri Bendell, Bloomingdales and others. It is also special to me for other reasons.

The shows that we took part in were the New York Prêt, London Fashion Week, Paris I, followed by Milan, then Paris II and lastly another show in New York at the end of the season. The trail was long and intensive and the samples were key to orders and follow-up publicity. Caroline and her sidekick Renée went to New York without me. I had been working on knitwear in a remote part of

Oil: 'distort' rib skirt and blood-red sheepskin jacket, 1986

Opposite page:
Oil: 'distort' wool sweater over embroidered fin waistcoat and leggings, 1986

Scotland, denim in the deepest East End and the prints just outside London. In those days the cost of launching a sample collection was about £15,000. It was months of legwork, communicating, costings, persuasion, drawing and pattern- and sample-making.

On the last day of the New York Prêt, Caroline and Renée had six collections from the stable of Amalgamated Talent bagged up around their feet and on trolleys. The dash for the airport was on, amid hundreds of others fighting their way to the same destinations. A man walked up to Caroline and asked in a foreign accent for directions and for a minute she turned her back on all the bags. He continued to act dumb and uncertain, and when she turned around again an accomplice had taken the bag with my collection and all the orders written over the four-day show. Caroline was devastated. No one knew more than her what effort it took to get these collections together in terms of money and time. When she finally called, she found it hard to tell me what had happened, that with her excitement at the great response to the collection and now her guilt for its disappearance.

I had ten days to do it all over again. I put the phone down and called all those who would be needed to put in every hour they had and accept payment terms way into the future. The collection was replaced on time – perfect – fuelled not only by the practical need for its re-emergence but also by the passion and will displayed by Caroline towards me.

Without doubt, the collection which turned my small company around was *Running Man* in Spring/Summer 1988. Lifted from a Greek

Zips as roses on sweatshirt dress and candlewick cotton coat, 1987

vase, his enormous phallus reluctantly removed, rows of identical men ran around hems, legs and waists of an otherwise simple collection. The Limited stores from America ordered the usual 1 – 2 – 1 ratio (one small, two medium, one large), only they meant 100, 200, 100 of each size. I watched Caroline's hand as it forced down the extra noughts on a column on the order pad printed too small to hold them. Doing our best to keep cool, as if the order were one of many this size, we shook as we discussed delivery dates, shipping and payment terms. I ran to a phone out of earshot to tell Ron the total. He asked me to repeat it four times, as if it were another language. In a sense, it was. This order was to break us out of the 'start-up' league. A manky calculator couldn't handle the noughts as we added the order up again (three times). When the dust had settled and we realized the capital we were going to need to finance the manufacturing, the trouble started. With a loan arranged at five on a Sunday afternoon, with a contact from The London Enterprise Agency (LENTA), an overdraft underwritten by a dear friend, a guarantee from my father and the presentation of a life-time to a shocked and yet to be convinced Barclays, we pulled it off. A cycle of not knowing if a season's orders would be financed began with regular six-monthly trips to the bank begging them to back recently acquired orders.

Caroline sourced a factory to produce the order at half the CMT (Cut, Make and Trim) price in the costings due to the volume, and three months of obsession started. Two months later, Ron and I were packing 180 boxes in a warehouse open to the snow in

Sweatshirt and lace zip dress from *Industrial Rose*, 1987

73

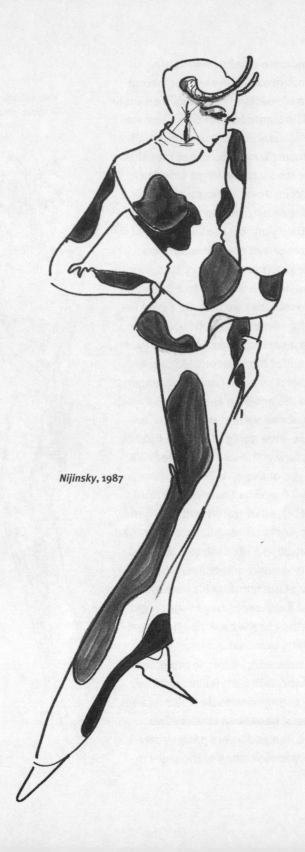

Nijinsky, 1987

Milton Keynes. Each night and morning I slept some and awoke to sweats: what if the fabric was flawed or late; if the grading was a fraction out; if the printers fucked up; if the factory went bust (which it almost did, courtesy of the Inland Revenue); or, worst of all, all the girls at the factory had their periods at the same time. When the shippers finally arrived on the last possible day, Ron and I were exhausted. Standing in the cold, we watched the truck pull away, holding our copy of the pick-up note. Motionless, with boxes and tissue still blowing in the background, frocks had restructured our lives. We were barely part-time parents and had willingly gone with the takeover.

A big and sudden jump in turnover is as much a thing to celebrate as it is a moment to fear. You could argue that it is precisely at such a time that investment should be sought, but an order like that arrives out of the blue in thirty minutes and with only two previous years of slow building trade before it, the rapid increase in our profitability was perceived by the professionals as a negative, an indication of risk. Such is England.

Our delivery to the States finally arrived and it only remained for us to chase our colossal payment. Pursuing an invoice from the Limited, you felt you were pestering a sleeping giant. The Limited is not so much a company as a City. The exchange rate was not in our favour and Caroline's barking power was stretched to the full. In the end, we lost £5,000 to the markets when the funds finally cleared. Carrying it to the bank was a moment to remember – as was the face of the cashier, who smiled at me ever afterwards.

Nijinsky, 1987

75

Besides America, it was the Far East and specifically Japan that had a great influence on sales in the early days. The first collection bought in any depth was Autumn/Winter 1988 *Victorian Rose*. At that time, Siebu of Japan had a love of what they perceived as wearable, eccentric clothes. A nation traditionally known less for innovation and more for the perfecting of it through technology responded to our fast-changing vitality. The exceptions to this are clearly Rei Kawakubo of Comme des Garçons and Issey Miyake, who, although different from each other, are seen by me and many others as highly innovative and masters of their craft.

The attraction for the Japanese was that young fashion design in the eighties sat as Portobello Road does to Harrods' designer floor. It gave an edge to their mainstay buying of Burberrys, Pringle and Aquascutum. Our designers provided them with an exciting pulse, best recalled through Bodymap and Richmond/Cornejo. It was through their initial buying patterns, and indeed the export market as a whole, that you could start to see how others regarded us from the outside. In market terms, it was also a lesson in what we had to do to keep them.

Although the sales of *Victoria Rose* were down from the *Running Man* collection, it wasn't so disappointing, considering the artificial boost the Limited order had given the season before. Around this time Amalgamated Talent Ltd was going through changes of its own. Having secured financial support from Marks & Spencer plc, NatWest, the Wellcome Foundation, Shell and more, Caroline was directed by her board to narrow down to the two she felt stood the best chance of longer-term financial success. Distraught, in a pub in Knightsbridge, she told me the bad news, which she had misinterpreted as failure.

The competition for her skills was falling away and I could see a path forward together. Along with

Indian Summer,
1987

Running Man collection, 1988

Karen Boyd, we formed a tripartite marketing tool known as Boyd and Storey. Our first shop and office base was in Newburgh Street, London W1, and, as with the others to follow, was designed by Ron. It was financed partly by the profits of the Limited order. Retail green, we threw ourselves into developing the special about ourselves, along with the wholesale side of our businesses, which remained financed individually.

Shortly after the commitment to Boyd and Storey, I asked David if I could leave Bellville Sassoon. It was a measure of his generosity that he had let me have time off to feel my way on early collections while still working for him. He always encouraged me to find myself, to follow the true path, whatever that was to be.

It is England's loss that the well-researched and powerfully driven Amalgamated Talent was on the whole perceived as a maverick idea that would rise or fall depending on Caroline's energies. What she was trying to do and say was for the greater good of enterprise, and profits of all sorts went on the whole unnoticed. As nomadic pursuers of success, each young designer stumbles over and through problems which could well be avoided with the existence of a collective umbrella firm like Amalgamated.

Boyd and Storey was my first taste of how much potential there was in fashion at that time. We were supported and encouraged by a love of all things British – Wedgwood, Liberty and Richard Branson. This was a time when opportunities were marked out as much by what we turned down as what we took on. In the early and mid-eighties there was no sense that it could burn itself out, least of all disappear up its own backside. There were even moments when the high street was vaguely threatened. We couldn't compete in terms of volume, but the customer, spurred on by us, was certainly demanding something new and more exciting. The results of taking this on board can still be seen today, as key high-street retailers find their balance between till sales and edge quality design.

Our first Boyd and Storey customer was Paula Yates, closely followed by Marie Helvin. And it was through women like these that my feeling for glamour was confirmed. At the same time, some of my greatest fans in those early days were transvestites, particularly on the New York scene. The Boyd and Storey collections grew organically, one out of the other, and a defined handwriting of Helen Storey started to emerge. As if to acknowledge this, in 1989 *Vogue* gave me five pages in one issue for my first season in this new set-up.

The noise and textures of ballet, experimentation at Kingston and Valentino, were coming together with a part of me that, by contrast, grew uncomfortable at the vision of woman I was creating. At times, she bordered on a 'slack tart' and the clothes relied greatly on the strength of the woman inside to portray her as anything more than that. In 1990, in a collection called *Wise Warrior Women,* through the use of sharp lines, chain and metal in contrast to Tri-cel, Fortuny pleating and silk, I was subconciously attempting to pull the two parts of me – a hard-nut woman and her melting and sexually available sister – together.

By now my list of stockists had risen to about fifty, and, with the greatest support coming from abroad, some true Helen Storey fans were emerging. I was getting used to the opening line from buyers each season: 'So what's Storey up to this time?' Knowing what I was up to was a fast-moving journey of discovery that had each collection accelerating bullet-like from the last. It is very dangerous to see yourself as the press do. However, it was only in talking to some of them that I could get the other half of the picture, normally supplied by the buyers and the hard realities of sell-through. My first editorial break of any meaning came in 1989. Interviewed by Marion Hume, then at the *Sunday Times*, I found myself questioning and verbalizing for the first time how and why I did it. At the beginning of recognition for fooling around with glamour, I was designing for that vital breakthrough from girl to woman, more commonly made accurate when designed by a man.

It was an exciting period and, looking back, the theatricality of my work was a perfectly timed moment, beautifully caught by

Sporting Life

Debbi Mason and Lucinda Chambers at the
start of British *Elle*. What I failed to recognize
was that somewhere in the mid-eighties
styling took over from design. The stylists
and their teams of creative support rivalled
the role of designer and some of us went
dangerously close to styling ourselves out
of a job.

Sporting Life

The second crucial press piece – the first
about me as a designer – came out at about
this time. Out of the blue, British *Vogue*
commissioned an interview and a shot by
Snowdon. Striding across a double-page
spread, I looked like someone he recognized
but I didn't. Most noted for its question mark,
the other side of 'Britain's next great hope?',
hope I remained, as for a long time I struggled for financial backing, despite
the growing media perception of Helen Storey the company, the designer and
the woman. Holding these two forces together, acknowledging that one exists
so that the other can too, is exhausting and to some extent I now consider it to
be counterproductive.

The last collection I did before finally getting to my Olympics (the catwalk)
was *Sporting Life*. In a catalogue of my life drawings, my need to get my
clothes into an arena of moving women hit its edge. Particularly with glamour
and sport as the influence, collections were now spontaneously designing
themselves into shoes, jewellery, bags – into a complete look. This look was
wasted when restricted to selling on a stand at an exhibition. The spirit to follow them through properly did not exist there, and neither did the backdrop
they required.

In those days you just did it – launched yourself into a catwalk show, a
creative coming out. This was a different league, and I had no inkling of what
would be needed to justify doing it. So in a hurry to get myself publicly defined –
away from my Signora training, my comparisons with Karen – my first show
was a spew of ranting ideas, too loud, too soon, too much.

8

Listen

with

Mother

My mother had a table in the corner of our living-room; it was her territory, her zone of 'Barbara alone'. Although chaotic, she knew where everything was. I realized it was a special place, most often used to make clothes for us or to draw flowers. It was a piece of identity she saved from the exclusive definition of 'Mum'. On the table sat a tank-like sewing-machine, knitting clobber, patterns and paper. A white wicker basket, once used to hold nappy-changing equipment, lay at the back against the wall. We weren't to touch anything. The table became a symbol to me in later years of what she had given up.

Her 'things' amounted to a handbag, nailfile, Worth perfume, purse and a bar of Fry's Chocolate Cream. Constantly pillaged by the children, they stand as a childhood-long reminder of how differently she wanted her girls to grow up. As young children we had only a part-time respect of what was special to her. We graffitied her life with our energy and noise. There was, however, one place where graffiti stuck: a blonde wooden pin box with steel pins that had shiny plastic heads – the first vivid colours I can remember – blood on top of the red ones, jaguar cream and Christmas-tree green. An early and mild rebellion, I stuck Biba stickers from the packaging of tights all over it.

I was twenty-six when I gave birth to Luke. Ron was still at Kingston, finishing part two of his architecture course, and I was dashing between Bellville Sassoon and the start of my first collections with Caroline. By the time my mother was thirty, there were four of us.

I ignored my pregnancy until, at seven months, I caught myself running after a bus between a lunch meeting with Caroline and getting back to Bellville's. The young child I was carrying kicked me hard for the first time and the bus emergency-stopped at the sight of my sprint. The women on board stared and the one who had had the clearest view tutted me into my seat. Inwardly, I wept at the now acknowledged change in me.

In my mid-twenties and fired up with my career, my pregnancy felt teenage. There was no one around, either old or new friends, who had this experience to help me through. Among them, I was always the first: the first to leave the country, to marry, to have a child, to get a mortgage. I was a lonely decade ahead of my peer group and I missed the reassurance of female experience.

On the day before Luke was born I sat upright in the bath and measured the shine on the outer curve of my stomach to my kneecap. A one-inch gap remained. I was enormous. My body had taken me over. I was surprised I had no control over it. Ron was as amazed and looked towards me in abstracted wonder.

I worked up until the birth, walking more slowly and staying shorter hours but still numbly trying to defy the inevitable. I felt my stomach was a foreign growth, had no instinct for what was on the inside. Those around me started to treat me as an art object, circling my body and staring in a way only those who can walk away can afford to do. I wasn't Helen; I was my pregnancy.

On a Sunday afternoon in November 1985 we sat in the flat under my parents' house. Ron was on the floor organizing receipts for our VAT return. His way of coping with the prospect of fatherhood while still at college was to grip the everyday and leave the rest to me. Until the first labour pains, this had been by mutual consent. Sorting the month of March, I said I couldn't go on. I was flushed, stuffed and starting to moan on the bed.

The Royal Free Hospital received us on Sunday at two in the afternoon. As I lay back for my first examination of many, a nurse smiled at my crotch. I had long given up trying to dress around my figure and had forgotten I was wearing Ron's Y-fronts. It didn't matter to her but was a measure of how far from myself I had reached.

At first my unstructured way of dressing suited pregnancy, but at six months I had grown beyond the biggest clothes I could find. Dressing my stomach with what was then available would have required a frightening transition. All I could see were frills at the neck and tents of lumpy or static fabric. Inevitably the hems would rise at the front to announce the ill considered garments. Towards the end I stuck to Ron's clothes and two pairs of trousers I swore I'd never wear again after the birth. Pregnancy is at odds with the part of fashion we find so hard to justify yet repeatedly condone anyway – thinness. These were isolated months inbetween the shape I knew and the shape I was at the very end. Dressing during pregnancy is especially hard for women who don't express their femininity through prettiness. Whoever designed the maternity wear I saw around must have imagined I spent the day posing next to foliage in gardens. The prettification of bumps still bewilders me. They are to me now best unhidden, when the form is accepted and held proud.

When my labour finally came, three weeks late, the pains were acute from the start; dilation did not match them. Three doctors later, I lay in a darkened room. The plan had been to go natural, but after fourteen hours I had nothing left to give and I sampled every drug and gas available. When I could no longer push, I was given an epidural.

Ron collapsed on to a birthing stool in the corner and at four in the morning the fourth doctor was summoned to help me. Our baby had monitors on its heart and head and whispers of Caesarean flickered round the room. Despite the hour, Dr Four came in with a fresh approach. The atmosphere in the room was anxious but, having been absent, he was unaffected by the last fourteen

hours, and came in singing Talking Heads' 'We're on the road to nowhere'.
A student followed him, having come to watch a problematic birth. The tune
triggered a smile and a push from nowhere. Forceps and a cut into me produced a head and a pair of shoulders. I felt down to the flesh, an erupted cav-
ern that was my lower body. The pull and the cut had me as meat, decked out
for slaughter or amputation. My whole body shifted with the tug applied to the
forceps. I thought the skull would crush. As the end was in sight, he handed the
forceps to the student and asked her if she'd like to have a go. Lying half up, half
down and with no familiar face or voice around me, Ron summoned his strength
to stand by my side. 'One last push, Helen.' I imitated what I thought it might
require. 'I want to die,' I said, and with a last controlled bellow he was out.

An alien with red hair – from neither Ron nor I – he was covered with every
fluid he and I could have produced. His throat was cleared, then he was
wrapped and left on my breast, and the room of eight emptied to the three of
us and silence. Stunned by the sudden lack of activity and the finality of it all,
I lay there wrecked. I felt guilt towards my baby and anger towards the birth
process. Even in labour a part of my mind was still living the next collection.
I had allowed myself no space, asked for no help. Labour pain was misinterpreted as nature's pay-back time. Bad at giving birth, I judged myself a joyless
and unappreciative little girl.

A few hours after Luke was born (Ron had gone home to get some rest and
spread the news), my curtains were whipped back and I was instructed to go to
a post-birth exercise class. During birth, obeying had been survival. I attempted
to stand on my epidural legs. In a bewildered state of mind, I groped my way
along the corridor walls into a roomful of women raring to reclaim their previous forms. A nurse rushed up behind me. 'You're not Jones, are you?' she said.
'No, I'm not,' I replied, and a wheelchair was whisked under my legs and I was
taken back to bed.

Some flowers arrived and were promptly delivered to the closed curtains in
front of me. I was to get them back by a process of elimination. The enclosure
opposite me stayed shut until the day my flowers were returned. The woman
inside cried day and night for two days. On the third day and in an effort by
the nurses to coax her back into the world, the curtains were brutally drawn
back to reveal both my flowers and an exhausted woman with a full-grown
beard. During some pregnancies the hormones play havoc – both male and
female hormones becoming active in unpredictable ways. While I was there,
she received no visitors and her face, in defiance of her female state, was
agony to her.

In the bed next to mine was a young girl in her teens. She winked at me often. I slowly realized that this was to secure my confidence, as her boyfriend was squatting under her bed each night. A social worker came to visit as he lay asleep under her one day. They spoke of her possibilities. She had nowhere to live, no money, and he had no job. She was found a room in a house in Camden Town and discharged herself back into the world.

At the end of the six-bed ward by the door I saw a familiar face come in. She waddled back to her bed, her baby in her arms. I later deduced that her labour had lasted two hours, with no drugs or gas, and that she had strolled straight back from the delivery room. Early the next day the boy I had had a crush on aged sixteen walked in – her brother. A pop star to be, I closed the curtains and hid: I needed to protect the last vision Jamie J. Morgan had had of me.

My mother and father came to visit, with a rescue package of Marmite sandwiches and satsumas. In my anger at the way the birth had gone, they felt welcome traitors: no tip-off, no hint of what I could have expected. My mother had had four of us. I had no idea such pain had been endured to have me. My brother Jake arrived and numbly, in silence, shoved a huge bar of Cadbury's chocolate in my hand.

Ron and his mother were in and out, but somehow always left just as Luke's crying became uncontrollable – the first glimpse of how energies were going to be split. The big visit came from the Gang. I recognized the sound of their group banter before I saw the giant pair of gold antlers come through the ward door. Champagne and glasses were spirited out of thin air, and cameras. Each of the six took their turn to hold Luke up to the ceiling, admiring a job well done. They left *en masse*, as they had arrived, leaving me exhausted and tearful.

To have a baby while acknowledging a part of yourself wants to or must work is to risk losing your best friend. The man who had been attracted to the strong part of me was now preoccupied with coping with his own reaction to Luke's birth. Disappearing into our separate emotional corners, we each struggled alone to make the transition that forges childless couples into parents.

The working mother, whether she goes back to work too soon or in her own time, faces double trouble, as a new deal must be struck with her partner in order to do so. I have watched my own and many of my friends' experiences since – a battleground, as biology excused the male the pace of change unavoidable in the female. A mother is by definition an altered woman. Many new fathers still take their time to budge and often at best just shift a little. Surprises come fast. I had assumed that the special in me before our baby would be preserved after his birth and that the journey back into the world of work would be a mutual hand-holding exercise. All the paths forward are new, and in young parents there is a period of readjustment as whether the father decides to become just that, a father; the mother, of course, has had no choice.

The first two years were the hardest. Within a few weeks I was back at work, breast milk squirting out of my shirt in the middle of an investment presentation to thirty besuited men; negotiating overdrafts while breast-feeding on the phone. It is, however, the little things that bulk large in the shaping of a young working mother and a new father. Time to sleep in and undisturbed baths are lost luxuries. With the loss of former times together, a layer of resentment builds up. One's best friend, supporter and fan becomes no longer good enough over a few weeks of disturbed sleep. As 'your turn' and 'my turn' take the strain, a half-hearted attempt, more often made by the female than the male, follows to try to hold on to the reasons why couples should stay together.

In the mid-eighties and in the early years of the business, what I missed most was obsession – the ability to see things through to the end, not leave half-way, hand over to someone else or just squeeze in. My obsessive qualities with my business were the first thing to go, as days became tightly timetabled and artificially structured towards pulling off the impossible.

The route of readjustment for Ron and me was slow, but we managed it. We ended up working together, a team effort to struggle, but with obvious potential in the business and the time and love we wanted to share with our son. The problems we encountered as new young parents were different from any previous worries experienced. In my need to work, I brought a new dynamic outside our frame of reference into play. I couldn't look back to see how my mother had coped as children had been her 'work'. None of my peer group was in the same position. In rapidly judging Ron as a father, I put him under great pressure to perform by insisting on both being a mother and working.

In my own father I saw an ease with babies and children that was an enormous relief. Even acknowledging that he could afford a detachment Ron didn't have, I was still unfairly disappointed that Ron couldn't produce the same easy confidence. Coming home from work in the first months, I would see my father and Luke watching the six o'clock news in the living-room. Luke would be propped up safely with cushions, displaying the attentive face of a far older man. Other times they would wander around the house, Dad talking to him and pointing out parts of paintings, or trees and birds in the garden. The best opportunity a man has of leaving boyhood, no matter what his age, is to become a father. In watching mine with Luke, I imagined a love for me that I received at an age too young to recall. I can see it in his face with any of his grandchildren: a love of their freedom from self-conscious acts, a joy at the unpredictable or perhaps it's the inevitable in them. From my mother, through her table and pin box, I felt she wanted more choice for us than she had had for herself. For my sister and me, there was encouragement to shape any future we wanted, to decide whether to be pregnant or not, to earn for ourselves and to aim as high and far as our eventual talents might allow.

My sister, Kate, is now a doctor of microbiology at Oxford. She has two children, Emma and Alex, and her partner, Jonathan, is away at sea often. She shares with me the dilemma that is the corollary of our mother's successful wish for our freedom: the need to be constantly juggling. Because what a woman gave up to have children can never be returned to; after children it is always a case of fitting things in alongside them.

It would be easier if mothering were enough. It used to be. Yet, in my mother, I saw a generation on the brink of wanting more. Her willing sacrifice to me was always being there, and showing me a world of choice; her love gave me the best chance to grab that world. In the gap that lies between the mother she was and the mother I became, there may be nothing more than a fight to redefine roles all over again. Perhaps the guilt that results from the struggle between my need to work and my desire to spend quality time with my child isn't worth it. If I could have looked into the future and seen the difference between what my career should have been and what it became, then maybe a table in the corner of my living-room would have been sufficient.

I have seen depression and since, felt it. Its relationship with creativity was part of an early landscape. It is something easily misunderstood by children. Luke asks me, 'Where have you gone?' Sometimes, it is only to a place in my head that decides if a button should be gold or silver. At other times, I have been caught wrecking my mind. The physical can reward his young mind's sense of loss at my departure. A game of football in the yard, a compensation for familiar moments when he must have felt invisible.

For women, there are no empires built without a cost to our children. I want the freedom to embrace and love both my son and my work, but to do so may mean that we have to consider a change for those years when children need us. If I had become a full-time mother, I would have been killing off a part of me that needed something different, and yet as I look back at bringing up Luke and working, I have had to accept a level of compromise few males would or could have done.

Our most innovative and creative years are paralleled by our most fertile. When I look and admire the work of others in my field, and beyond, that work has usually been created either by a man or by a woman not actively involved with childcare. There are exceptions, obviously, but the brilliance of the woman who is actively involved can usually be traced back to the fact that shortly after having had children she handed them over to others in one form or another. In creative terms, the female years rightly given over to children are in consequence lost to the active decision-making processes in our society. One of us has to lose. The middle ground of doing both tears at the centre of me daily. The solution found to avoid this situation – speedily having child number two – is baffling to me. He or she is often created out of forgiveness of the man's behaviour first time around and the female's acceptance that this is as good as it's going to get anyway. Somewhere through the strain of parenting and earning a living, it is now clear that certain groups of men and women have become fundamentally disappointed with each other. We are not the mothers theirs may have been and they are not the fathers we need them to become.

The working mother is exhausted from constantly picking up the slack, just as the fathers are by our constant pestering to remind them of it. Many women are happier coping as single parents, truthfully defined, rather than having to feel that that is exactly what they are within a marriage. In the isolation and anger of the status quo, neither parent gets much save protection from the agony of change itself. Feminism, as a movement, does not hold the answers and nor, on its own, should it. Alienated by ranting feminists from an early age and at odds with their hatred of men, feminism as it chose to present itself during my formative years has held nothing for me.

I am no follower of written feminism and all my thoughts are based on experience and not the word or changing philosophy of others. However, behind the generation which screamed, there now stands a quieter line-up. Having undoubtedly benefited from the first charge, these women are different, and I am one of them. We have in our hands an inherited sword held over a seal-pup generation of men. We survey the changes forged on our behalf at a time when men quietly fear that women can rule the world. The female in the workplace is uniquely driven – by either the energy and go-for-it spirit she can afford by not having children or the demonic speed and concentration she has to apply to her allotted time slots when those that she has are being looked after or are in school. Both ways, this energy, however focused, is formidable in the face of many men, whose historical working pace in recent years has been made possible with the safe knowledge that mother is doing her unpaid stuff back home. Men have got the message but have never had the luxury of time to contemplate their approach to change. They have been working not thinking, earning not philosophizing. In the world of business there are too many just getting on with it, and not enough experienced people paid to ask why. Their hackneyed suits prop up a way of working that exists purely and simply because it has for so long. The females at the top level of businesses or on boards are often better than their male counterparts; they have had to be just to get there. This on the whole untackled dilemma divides women into those willing to run the risks of doing both and those for whom a career or motherhood is all.

The workplace needs to change, not just in response to mothers with the spur of biology behind them. The necessary readjustments could benefit the family enormously. Part-time is not a lack of commitment, it is a balancing of life. A system that refuses to make determined and long-term changes on behalf of working mothers will ultimately be a poorer place for it.

Among the men who have changed in an honourable effort to redress the present balance, there is now confusion. For the women who choose to be mothers and work, there are few choices but to accept compromise, job-shares or the prospect of boarding school. The great majority of men still believe that the world of business should go round without an abundance of the female touch. Of the women at decision-making level, I suspect many still forgo or put off having children in order to keep on track with their male colleagues. How much greater women's business skills might be for the experience of being also a respected and cherished mother. The energy of feminism directed specifically at males should now fade. Gender has become our decoy to progress. We should instead jointly refocus our stamina and skills towards a humanizing of the home and the workplace for all. Both sexes unarmed, a hard-fought but negotiated *inequality* will always exist.

9
Rage

Unprompted, the first instinct among strong women photographed in my work has often been to spit. If ever proof were needed to demonstrate that clothes can deliver a message, it is here. The silent and successful transmission of an old cargo of mine – an energy that, thankfully, no technology could ever hope to mimic.

Rage marked the beginning. My first catwalk show received as much praise as it did damnation: from 'what Britain's been waiting for' to 'an apocalyptic mess'. But liked or disliked, with many of the big British names on the move – Hamnett, Galliano, Westwood and Ozbek – *Rage* made a noise at a time when a certain stillness was in the air.

Putting the collection together was a nightmare. I soon realized that what sells would put the audience to sleep and that the newsworthy and edgy stuff would be impractical and unprofitable to manufacture. I learned fast the first time around and my lessons had paid off by the time the next season arrived. For *Rage*, in a room which could comfortably hold two, there were at one point ten people, cutting patterns, sewing, divorcing, styling, casting models and having supposed secret affairs. A tension I could bring nowhere near the surface almost had me over my edge. Invariably, there is always too much in a first catwalk show. The need to yell rather than simply announce is a seemingly unavoidable urge, especially in the young. The *Present Times* collection (1991), by contrast, was designed and worked on in a large rented space in Kingly Street, London W1. Up three flights of stairs but isolated from the day-to-day, a

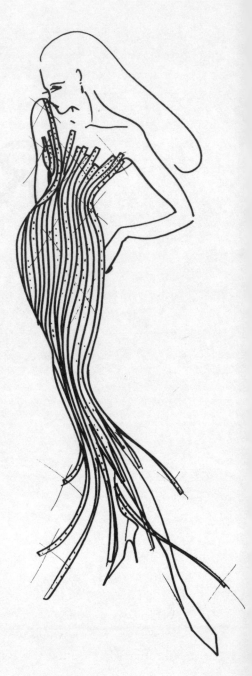

New York Skyline dress, with hand-sewn diamanté strips, 1991

tight team produced what I still consider to be my best work. Finally, after seasons of no coordination, I had machinists, Mark, my pattern-cutter, my darling Helen Bailey to assist, Sharlot and some peace all under one roof.

There should be a Sharlot in every workroom. In the best fashion houses they are bred from generation to generation – the weft to our warp as designers. When they are silent, but most often over chatter, one can glimpse their effortless skill. The years of perfection in any couture house can be seen in the rheumatoid knuckles of women.

Silk chiffon does not want to be hemmed, it never has. It has a wriggling quality found large in the nappy-changing of a defiant child. Rolling a spliff of silk is a process almost invisible to the eye, a play with gravity against the knot that allows the slither and slide. The hold and strain are born by the knuckle, the ligament strung up to the wrist, allowing

Stairway to Heaven ballgown worn with moulded fur bodice, *Present Times*, 1991 a needle's prick to remain light. The eye chooses a strand on which all other threads will depend. In Sharlot's hands chiffon will obey, can follow a course of miles; never is the suffering transported to the edge. The work that flows behind has stitched in it a mother's love, a selfless chance to see the unfinished completed as wind.

There is a magical time when the inner team can telepathize a collection – when you know it's right with eyes, not words; when her or his decision is as any one of us would have made. It takes place when much of the designing is done but there is still a gap for 'her' wings to unfold. Where all the differing elements start to take a unified shape, as a child to come, you wait for 'her' unknown face: a unique mix of all who have put into her. One collection will always be emerging as the previous one is being manufactured. The one that is being creatively finished with still demands a great deal of attention after the event. *Rage* was being manufactured in Cornwall by my new and surrogate family, Barbara, Darren and Peter Cowperthwaite, while *Present Times* was being developed. New to this game of trying to please both buyers and press, *Rage* had everyone in one, as it was virtually impossible to manufacture. By the time we had satisfied every buyer's individual wishes on an order, there were more than 160 styles and the company simply could not produce them all. Our mistake was to even attempt it. What we had created was somewhere dangerously between ready-to-wear and couture. As the chaos of *Rage* continued, I used all the mistakes I had made in it to keep *Present Times* clean and straightforward. As a result, that collection's themes still continue as lead stories in today's editorials.

Present Times' energy came from nowhere specific but through relying on instinct. With the previous collection styled beyond recognition, in this one the clothes alone told me what to do: when to leave them, when they needed some sisterly edge. For the first time I consciously listened to a voice with no face. I felt for couture. I missed its possibilities – the crafts and support that must surround a designer for its life to be real. So I turned to the truth of what was to hand. Council rubbish bags became a ball skirt, floating with a static and flow only polythene and net can agree. The animal heads which prompted so much coverage in the press were the result of a long evening's discussion with Ron – my rambling partner in life's more creative moments. He claims the idea was his and I, indisputably, that it was mine. In the past, in these brainstorming sessions there have been times when the only point on which we could agree was that the other's recollection was wrong. The hair was by Vidal Sassoon, the twenty girls split between shaven heads and locks of coiffured abundance; the make-up by Lesley Chilkes, a moon-dust and blood-lipped creation. I worked with Shelly's on the loafers, which floated on clear Perspex wedges, and throughout the collection commercialism lent itself so inventively, and perhaps rarely, to the experimental.

In satisfying the theatrical in me, the catwalk was fast becoming an addiction. The job of selling, however, without its distraction, had to go on. The stand shows in New York, and later on with the help of our US agents, Showroom 7, grew to be one of the most important on a season's circuit. Agents are essential to growth and finding the right ones is an important decision. At our peak we had six around the world, each presenting the same collection in a different way. In Showroom 7's hands a collection could be dramatically re-invented, their knowledge of the US market built up over many years through the vital eyes and strong mouth of Karen Ericksen. Adapting a range to the territorial differences between our English vision and another's needs is key to a collection's global appeal.

Though Britain and the US share the same language, we do not share the same body shape. My instinct for clothes of fit and definition put me in the front line of all they feel compelled to control, hold back and reshape. In designing with flesh in mind, we met some extraordinary women and buyers. I realize, having tasted some of New York and LA, that these ladies of eternal youth are quite commonplace, but for the then young British eyes these early versions were a shock.

One of our first hotel shows was at the Plaza, just off Central Park. Exhibitions were strange. Sitting in your room, having temporarily decorated some of your personality on to its walls, you sit and wait, almost whore-like, for someone to cross your intimate threshold. There is no sense of passing trade, as in an open exhibition, but more an 'in your face' unavoidable intimacy, making both a good sell and a rejection highly personal. The Americans are very used to this way of working, and you either adopt it or drop it.

The room you sell in is also the room you sleep in and often don't leave for the entire day. A night-time vision of New York was almost all I ever experienced, as the journey from long immigration queues into a yellow cab and hotel room was the transatlantic tunnel for selling ideas into the States. The only other time I could see New York was in the very early morning. The magical half-light time as day pulled through night too early for home folk but it was lunchtime for us. Pax Café was a favourite haunt. Breakfast that looked like lunch was shovelled down, before striding to the edge of Central Park in the sun and fog and then back to the hotel room for day two.

Jet-lagged, comforted by onion soup and permanently dehydrated from the hotel air, you awaited your punters. First around the door one particular morning was a giant pair of nostrils. Her face was pulled, chin and cheeks up, I assume over and under her red hair. She wore a wig which might have been lent to her by a window display team and her make-up, with a life of its own, resisted her face. I jumped when I saw her. She was clearly used to this response. If you had taken off her head and ignored the reptilian hands, then she was an identikit version of the daughter who came around the door next. Both wore tight Lycra pants and flat black pumps, and as if in a Russian doll sequence yet another female appeared, identically dressed, around fourteen years old. This ageing necklace of females thumbed through the clothes in silence. I threw glances at Caroline, but professionalism was flowing and a full explanation of the range and its history came out. I suppose by silent agreement one of us was allowed shock and the other the sales pitch. We began to chat, the sort of conversation which we would continue to have again and again over the years with many other buyers.

Mad Max waistcoat,
Present Times, 1991

The conversation I really wanted to have would have involved asking, why the cosmetic surgery. I wanted to talk to her eyes, not the black holes of grease. Protected by the irreversible, she was unapproachable. In that trio were three generations of women from the same family and yet to some extent they were one: the youngest could look forward to the physical certainty of her years to come, the grandmother could look back at the beauty she must once have had and the lady in the middle was both haunted and taunted, by the youth she was leaving and the age she would become.

If day one had been a lesson in the American vision of lasting beauty as procured by cosmetic surgery, then day two was my eye-opener on American breasts. I had come

up with the idea of putting stretch fabric on the back of leather in order to create good fit and lower the price of the garment. Walking forward, you are
leather-clad; from the back, a sleek black and perfect fit-to-you woman. It is
often the case that the buyer might share a similar figure with her customers,
so in place of our house model they themselves would try garments on. On
this day 'Miss Beverly Hills' put on a leather half-and-half waistcoat. Where
the bust lies this side of the Atlantic, it appears waist level on the other.
Where ample shape over and around the bust will do here, a cleavage to be
genuinely mistaken for a backside is forced up front over there. A glance back
to Lara, our model, and back again to Miss Beverly Hills had me confused.
Who was real here? Whose figure do I believe
and trust? Lara stared at the splendour of this

Rish Rubbish jeans and Fortuny
pleat T-shirt with Lycra back,
Present Times, 1991

frontal arse and the buyer cried out in disap-
pointment:

'Helen, you must understand that every
woman has a bust job and a nose job and her
hips and tush are sucked. Get real if you want
to sell here. This is real.' And then, pointing to
Lara, 'And that, charming though it is, is *not*.'

I ended up doing two versions of everything she bought, and she bought a lot. To
this day I still see these pumped-up women
photographed at various do's, looking inexplicably authentic and, as perceived by them,
luckier than us.

There are three types of buyer and not much
in between. In America, as with many other
things, the types can be seen to extreme.
The first know nothing but, pretending to
know all, they thumb the rails and whisper.
Often overwhelmed, they leave the room or
place a personal order for their niece. The
second know a dangerously small amount
and will wherever possible attempt to
redesign your collection. Their entrance is
usually with a drawn-out 'Hi, how're you
doing, honey, show us your line.' Half an

hour later, unless you have got them to laugh, drink or eat, they're off to waste another poor designer's time next door. The third probably work for a store beginning with the letter B: 'Boy, do they know their stuff.' On occasions, as they arrive at the head of a team of three or four, 'Good morning' was reduced to a grunt as their schedule permitted little else. They would go through the rails, passing back their selection to their number two. In New York in particular, the faces I remember most were those 'sell-through' skins, drawn across faces that seemingly lived or died against their square-footaged performance. In our case, however, there was a fourth set of buyers. Known to me as Roz, Heidi, Gapu, Kevin, Carlos, Henry and Andria, they bought through an instinctive passion, never lost touch with gut reaction and took risks where others wouldn't. They were the ones who pumped my heart.

Backstage after *Present Times*, those people who make or break you queued to congratulate me. As each respected face fought its way towards me, I knew I had got it right, one of those rare moments when love is felt the same. During that year, and as a result of that particular collection, I was voted Most Innovative Designer of the Year and also nominated for Designer of the Year. It was 1991 and the only way was up.

Having left Boyd and Storey in 1988 in an effort to define myself independently in terms of image and corporate identity, in 1990 what was left of the original Amalgamated Talent became Coates and Storey Ltd. What marked this new phase was an emphasis on catwalk shows, and all the

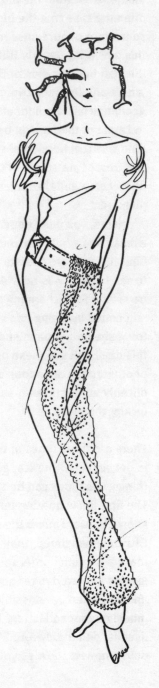

Women in Love, 1992

changes that have to take place as a result.

We moved studios again to design and develop *Women in Love* in a giant disused old engine room in Kentish Town, north London. For this collection I took six strong females: Frida Kahlo, Alice in Wonderland, Second-hand Rose, Jezebel, Joan of Arc and Mary. The collection, however, was too ambitious for our set-up, although it was one of the most beautiful.

The sixth-month trail of one catwalk collection after another was taking its toll, as the company had to do so much to keep up with the work the name was generating. In our case, and I imagine it must be true for others also, the success or failure of individual shows would be perfectly reflected by the economic and structural climate in which the collections were created.

If *Women in Love* was one of my favourite collections, what followed was probably our ugliest. *Dreams and Reality* (Autumn/ Winter 1992) was a pig. Poorly fabricated, badly made, aimed at no one in particular, not surprisingly it flunked. I could feel it at the design stage, as Mark asked me more and more questions that I couldn't answer. Sketches that made no sense just sat on the wall like wet

Jezebel, *Women in Love*, 1992

doodles pretending to mean something. God, it's a foul feeling to know that you've lost it, and worse still to commit to displaying it in public. To be fair to myself, there was starting within me a feeling of misplacement as a designer. It showed its face in the Second-hand Rose character from the season before. A woman who borrowed from old collections, mixed other designers' clothes with her own and made what should have been a feather boa out of rags herself. She didn't want a label, she wanted her personality back. What did it mean for me if she succeeded? If she got sick of the prices we had to charge and wouldn't swallow a head-to-toe look any more. Rose was telling me something: the design equivalent of that glib saying, 'Get a life!'

In 1992 we bought a building and a shop on the King's Road in Chelsea and launched with a range called *2nd Life*. In homage to Rose's pestering, I started sourcing second-hand clothes from Flip's warehouses in Covent Garden. I wallowed in a childhood definition of heaven: hundreds of bales of clothes from the thirties to the present day, there to discover and revamp. Like a thirteen-year-old back in jumble-sale mode, spotting treasure through the fat backs of old women, I had found something to reinspire me, something that might also address what I perceived to be one of the problems specific to fashion designers.

The grand idea once again constrained by space, money and time, was to develop *2nd Life* into an entity of its own. The labour force was to comprise students or qualified and out-of-work

Dreams and Reality, 1992

Dreams and Reality, 1992

fashion designers. The vision was to produce individual one-off, cheap and multi-sized garments. Seasonless and forever changing, time could be pillaged at will and in having our own retail outlets, I could respond to new moods as they hit. Despite the recession, our business in 1993 was at its peak and profitable. Flip in turn sponsored *Angelheart* (Autumn/Winter 1993), which put many of these ideas on the catwalk. Either badly explained by 'us', or misunderstood by 'them', the second-hand theme was rejected and perceived as both 'grunge' and a signal of disrespect to the designer's craft.

It is noticeable that throughout my collections those most commercially successful were rarely photographed. Indeed, the best-selling dress of my career, in production for five years, was never photographed at all. In sharp contrast, the collections least commercially successful received significant coverage in magazines and newspapers. In each stylist there is a designer, in each designer a stylist. At times we meet in a middle ground, share a vision which we commit to, even if the commercial demand for it is unknown, perhaps doubtful. But we are still in an age where the style sections of big magazines are brokering the future as much as the designers themselves can.

To push the point too far, as occasionally I do, the finale in *Angelheart* used ten vintage patterns from couture masters of the past. All the garments were made out of cloth that cost less than £5 per metre, yet still looked special. My point, although missed, was to show that beautiful clothes need not cost a fortune or come from a designer each season. It was also to further the debate around questions of why designers churned out what they did and who it was ultimately for.

To express an instinct outside the arena of clothes on a catwalk is a dangerous thing, or if not dangerous then pointless. To use the catwalk to comment on a sense of future redundancy for our breed begs no questions of those who in their minds are already on the plane to Paris to sit through another eighty-five shows the following week: 'Just give us the frocks, Storey, and fuck the message!'

10

The
Undesigned

There have been times when the only thing that was clear was that nothing else was going to be. This was one of those times. It started with a scent – a scent, not a smell – giving only a hint of what was to come. It could mislead, intrigue and shock. It lingered. Damp and sweet, it reminded me of childhood rolls in September leaves; it awoke us in the middle of three consecutive nights.

Ron's familiar but distorted face came around the door of Luke's room as we played on his bed one early Sunday morning. The right eye had blown out and a swelling like a child's finger lay under the skin, pulling at the side of his nose and pointing diagonally to his jaw. We called in a reluctant GP. I cross-examined him as to how much more serious this was supposed to get before they did something about it. If it had been a cyst, why hadn't it been treated? There was a dumb and uncomfortable shrug. It was Sunday, it was Easter, he wasn't sure. He gave Ron some antibiotics and left.

Back at work on the Tuesday, that sweet smell stayed up my nostrils, neither pleasant nor foul but so strong I expected it to be commented upon. The unnameable fear I imparted to no one and I carried around this newness, as disturbing, perhaps, as an undiscovered colour might be on the eye. I can remember walking up the shabby stairs at work after the Easter break and coming face to face with Caroline, hers already holding the tight, pale skin only an overdraft, £10,000 over its limit, can do. Despite the battles of the day having already commenced, she dropped the 'Hello' for 'What's happened?' I reported that Ron was ill and we carried on. The day continued as Ron, with little hearing, not much sense of smell and obscured vision in one eye, struggled to concentrate on whatever screamed out for attention first, his desk piled high with wads of trouble. I don't think I could have halted the pace of life to which we had committed ourselves if I had wanted to. Ron, Caroline and I – none could have known where it would take us, but Caroline and I have often wondered why it wasn't one of us instead of him.

The next morning, feeling that we'd been fobbed off with antibiotics for long enough, we controlled an otherwise explosive entrance into our GP's surgery. She must have been able to sense the trouble we were having, as my speech was delivered in very few words: 'I think the hospital is where we should be. I think you should call them now.' Nothing more was said. She stared at Ron's eye and then back at me, acknowledging the seriousness for the first time.

By midday we were at the ENT clinic and a cheerful doctor with a fresh, seen-it-all approach assured us that this was a blockage at the top of the nose and that a scan would easily confirm it. I remember being in front of a painting of a

Recycled Amish
blankets worn
with silk chiffon

Susie Bick, Luke & me

Sequined lace-up corset

A touch of couture for a fiver

Scroll sequined tabard

Left: 'Edith' at her best!

Red planet dress – 'Mars'

Patent arch
ass jacket with
beast pencil
skirt

Backside in lace

'On a purple morning':
rose petal padded silk
organza coat

Moulded rubber and
silk crêpe dress

Bag-bra

Susie Bick as 'Death', *Rebecca*, 1994

Golden 'wide boy'

Eve and elephant. *Elle*, 1994

'God of War' coat.
Marie Claire, 1995

Luke & me, 1991,
by David Scheineman

Ron, Luke & me. Tom Miller for *Elle Decoration*, 1989

tiger as he spoke. That tiger stayed in my mind throughout the months to come. It was an innocent warning of the strength we were to need; of all the things we would have to learn so quickly; of how to sense danger for ourselves. And, just as Ron's back had been turned away from it as the doctor spoke, it was a signal that our journeys were to be both bound and yet separate.

Hospital art can never quite convince. While attempting to distract you, it also serves as a reminder that you are in a place where you have no control; that your body has gone one way and has made no deal with you about returning to health; and that you must entrust yourself to strangers.

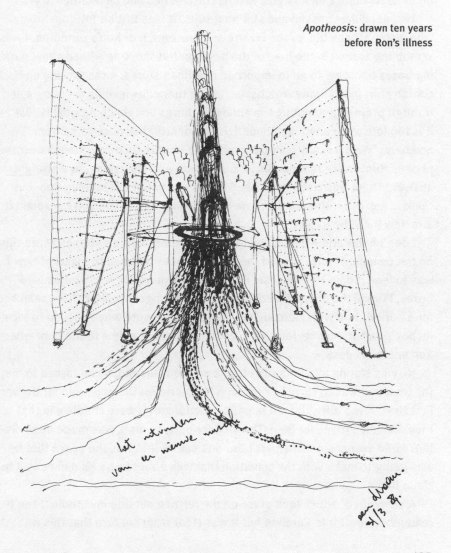

Apotheosis: drawn ten years
before Ron's illness

The scan results came back and Ron and I trooped off to ENT, still protect-ed by innocence and lulled by the patience needed to get through any hospi-tal appointment. Lesson one: how to tell black areas from grey. What looks healthy to the common eye works in reverse on a scan. A new doctor stood in command as ours hung back in deference to higher status. It was explained to us that they were still not worried but, due to the extent of the grey area, per-haps a biopsy would be a good thing.

On 15 April, 1993, Charing Cross Hospital was pleased to inform us that a bed was available, and on 19 April they pulled out a chunk of the swelling and sent it off to Haematology for analysis. Ron was discharged and he returned to work.

Two deadlines passed and still no results. It was British Telecom finally who were responsible for the bizarre announcement of Ron's condition. I was scrabbling around in the hole of the basement at the King's Road shop, pack-ing boxes of orders to go to important American stores. I was tucking up each chiffon shirt individually with tissue, laying them down while chanting sell-through prayers, and noting the annoying things you do about quality just as it is too late to do anything about it. An unidentifiable voice came from nowhere: 'Well, it really isn't our practice to impart such information over the phone.' Ron's voice replied: 'But it's about me and I'm asking for a straight answer.' There was a slight pause. 'You have a malignant tumour, Ron, but there is more to it than that and we really would like to see you to explain it and how it can be treated.'

I don't know and never asked how many other people's phones heard this on the communal mike around the building, but it marked the start of how I was to learn about this disease. Rummaging around old rails and unused boxes, I found the phone that delivered the message. I couldn't have searched for a buried child with more vigour. I am not quite sure why I needed to locate its position but, having done so, I ran three steps at a time to the floor where Ron sat at his desk.

He was staring at a Polaroid of Luke on the wall, and, as he turned to me, the look that was to carry him through his battle for life appeared for the very first time. It is a difficult look to paint. Fractions of it were childlike in that they appealed to me for help. The broader part, though, was made up of dis-tance and suspension. The part I couldn't see at first was the peace that he was going to make with the condition that was about to try its damnedest to claim him.

A powwow of shock took place on the terrace outside my studio. I can't remember how I told Caroline but it was clear from my face that this was serious. We hung on to the wall and looked over a pretty square in Chelsea flooded with sun. Where should bad news happen? Caroline said, 'I think you should go home' – an understandable yet somehow useless response. Equally useless was mine, about who would handle what shit at work. Ron's response was silence. We passed around this lethal knowledge. What do you do when you are told you have got cancer? Go home and put your feet up?

My second response was to call my father. 'I have to call my dad,' I told them both, and went back to the phone that still sat among the clawed and chucked-about debris in the basement. Dad answered the phone. 'Dad, it's malignant. It's a tumour.'

I had never said the word 'malignant' before. To this day I often mix it up with 'benign'. The conversation was short, as I soon realized I didn't know what I was talking about – a strange sensation, to feel you are in deep but not know in what. But I think Dad knew, and as with the look on Ron's face at the news, the tone of my father's voice was to become the sound of survival: it was how I would measure my sanity; he became my translator, the interpreter of reality. I was to find a love for my father I might never have felt but for the threat that his own life was drawing to a close.

On 10 May my diary listed the following:

> 10.30, INTERVIEW WITH HIGH FASHION (JAPAN).
> PRINT OUT HOLIDAY COLLECTION PRICE LIST.
> BRING IN GOLD DRESS.
> GIVE STUDENT ADVICE ON CAREER.
> DROP OFF DENIM TO STONEWASHERS.
> CANCEL HAIR APPOINTMENT.
> PRODUCTION MEETING WITH LYNNE.
> FINANCE MEETING WITH CAROLINE.
> STOCK-TAKE FABRICS.
> ISSUE DOCKETS TO COATES VIYELLA.
> INLAND REVENUE RESPONSE TO PAYMENT SCHEDULE ???
> PACK SAMPLES, SHOWROOM 7 USA AGENT.
> SOURCE REPLACEMENT VELVET.
> PHOTO-SHOOT WITH THE TELEGRAPH.
> GET TO SEE VOGUE SHOTS.
> CHASE MARIA.
> CLEAR THE STUDIO.
> BACK TO HOSPITAL WITH RON.

'It's called high-grade T-cell lymphoma,' said the doctor, 'and it's the one to have. We'll send you to Dr Leslie in Radiotherapy and see you in three months.' The closing remark: 'It will melt away.'

The diary now looks ridiculous. As time wore on, Caroline took the world of work off my shoulders and I entered the world of Charing Cross Hospital. I developed an ever-changing relationship with the building and the people in it. Some days I felt timid towards it and others angry; in the end I became reverential. I saw the circumstances in which doctors and nurses worked and realized I knew nothing of hard work or of patience or of listening.

After a short while, Caroline asked me to ask Ron if he wanted the business to carry on. Strange that I should accept the role of messenger on this one, but I knew exactly what she meant. The build-up to Ron's illness had been fraught with stress as the three of us, individually driven, struggled to survive and maintain the tenacity needed to find that elusive finance. He answered quickly and said, 'Without question.'

His reason, I can now see, was that, in order to survive an illness of this type, you make a pact with the outside world as it was before it happened. This becomes a way home and allows you to summon the strength to face what lies ahead.

We have a thousand billion cells in our body and each one is supposed to know what it is doing: when to multiply, when to diminish. Cells that don't commit suicide are as dangerous as those that decide to multiply. I'm not sure which type made up Ron's disease but it became for me a second person and I spontaneously made it male. Its host was gentle – a disease could not wish for a fairer battleground. Ron took treatment in the moment. On the hour, blood was taken, and a screen broke it down one hour later into a five-pattern result which became the barometer of his condition, his state of mind and his chances.

After a short time my skill at judging situations, at overhearing and interpreting what was said, became an exhausting addiction. My father and I trawled for information, both that we should and should not know. The way it was delivered was, at first, as much as most people might want. Instinctively we always dug deeper. For me, understanding the alien was a crucial part of trying to make a deal with it. In reality, all we could do was to keep Ron with us, as the deal had to be made through him.

Ron used to windsurf and one summer in Greece we spent three months on a beach. It was just after leaving college and, seeing no space for the likes of me in London at that time, we bummed out on the tip of Corfu. In surfing, he felt the air very well. He sensed how to get it, hold it, push it, ride the edge of its energy where it could snap and spin your body, dumping you back in the sea. He maintained that if you learned how to hang your body between the elements there was, magically, no effort required at all – no battle, just speed. Uninterrupted, he often looked as if he had left himself, conscious only of the achievement when he dumped down his board and sail on the beach, as a conductor might his baton at the end of a concert. Now, years later, he drew on the same instinctive part of his nature to pace himself through his illness. Cancer, however, was the roughest of seas: taunting and provocative, luring and ferocious, it challenged Ron's ability to 'ride'. It was as if he were surfing at night, with no definition of land or light visible; the disease had a clear advantage.

Talents, developed as a child in a big school, were now called upon. My ability to identify the enemy in a crowd, the result of prolonged and terrifying experiences in the corridors between classes, proved useful. In effect, it was a gift and perhaps a skill essential in all professions where success is guaranteed primarily through the insecurity of others – to hold one full conversation while all the while concentrating on picking up the detail of another.

One night, not long after it had started, we were in the radiotherapy department. There were no other patients. Dr Glazer, Head of Radiotherapy, was our magician. He sat before us making conversation. Behind him stood his assistant, whose job it was to programme in his percentages and waves – a radiotherapeutic prescription of the amount of radiotherapy to be given and where. A wall partially blocked the view of Ron and the technician saw only me. When I got home that night, after three hours of holding my secret to myself in front of Ron, I went through what I had heard on my own.

Looking at Ron's scan, the technician turned to Glazer and said, 'This is untreatable.' Dr Glazer's face shifted. He looked at me very quickly to see if I had made the connection. Suddenly he vaulted over the back of the seat. 'Get in that room!' he shouted. 'Get into this room now! How dare you say that in front of a patient!' He pulled her round. No warning had been given to prepare her for the encounter. I heard a curtain ripped back and the shock of a body being pinned against a wall. Glazer spoke again, still in earshot. 'This boy's going blind in his right eye and he has a tumour spreading like wildfire. I haven't been in this profession for twenty years for you to tell me what's treatable and what's not.'

There followed several minutes of conversation about hot spots, degrees, approach, leverage, capacity and a lot of jargon which went over my head. Silence. I heard only an electrical buzz throughout my body. The urge to vomit was unbearable. I attempted to carry on talking to Ron in order to distract him. There was no need. Protected by a developing deafness, he looked at me with a smile as if to indicate the semi-comical vaulting of Glazer over the back of the seat. Strange how humour can follow shock. As Glazer reappeared, as if from stage left, straightening his hair and jacket, he walked ahead and past us, stopping briefly to wish us good-night.

I imagine that Ron started off as just another of the 3,000 patients Glazer saw every year. I know each of us would like to think our treatment is special or individual, but I truly believe that Ron's illness tested Glazer's genius to the full. He was short, well groomed and delivered his words in a camp Jewish style. I developed a need to know of his whereabouts rather like a child's need for its mother. He ruled his kingdom. His charisma was wards thick; his aura on approach had nurses and orderlies shaking minutes before he arrived. He was invariably followed by a team of doctors who had much pride to swallow for the price of watching him work. He had one face when he entered a room for a patient, and another for his team. I had the privilege of seeing both.

Ron's mother, Anna, came to stay. I had talked frequently to Ron's parents during the muddling diagnosis period and it was with enormous relief that I heard she was coming to England. I was still taking Luke to school, working every morning, rushing to the hospital, picking Luke up from school, going to the hospital with Luke every evening and then coming home again: a wretched dance that had me lost. I wore so many faces during that time. Life would have been intolerable if the A-team hadn't spontaneously come together.

Anna is an immaculate woman, quiet and unassuming. She has played a background role for years; all her life she has supported those who, on the face of it, don't look as if they need it. She does and will tolerate anything in the name of love, and her ability to work and keep life together was difficult to match. The flat was kept spotless. Luke was entertained. We were fed and for six months solid she kept midnight vigil over her son. She is Dutch and speaks fair English, but needed little of it at our most intimate moments. On the Hammersmith roundabout after a few months had passed, she asked me if I was ready for his death; we weighed it up, passing it from front seat to front seat. When Ron was readmitted for the fifth time, this time to go into isolation, she looked from her chair by his bed, her son bound in blankets, bald, eyes shut, then looked at me. She was, perhaps, the last of us to realize how ill he was.

A number of stages lay ahead as the process of attempting to cure Ron's illness started. The first was the making of a mask to protect those parts of his head and face that were not to be subjected to radiotherapy. The man who did this was very calm and quiet; he needed all his skill to prevent Ron panicking. Ron's face was covered with plaster and two straws were inserted in his nostrils so he could breathe. What the mask-maker didn't realize was that Ron could not breathe, as one nostril was blocked by the tumour. Ron started to struggle. I was asked to leave the room during this process. Visions of arms and chairs being grasped in panic flashed through my mind. Useless, sitting outside, I heard muffled hums and gasps. I knew there would be many situations like this to come. I started to create an inner world, one that somehow shared Ron's experience, and in defiance of it developed a confident face that had to greet him after each episode of any treatment. The carer's face tries at all costs to show no fear. The troubled part that dares not react in the presence of the sufferer goes somewhere else – to the pillow that night, to a time some way ahead when the sufferer is not around to see it. We look for a safety zone, a place where it is okay to let surface whatever we are keeping back. Intolerantly, what I truly couldn't stomach was the 'he'll make it through' brigade. This avoided the pain so completely, letting the purveyor of this knowledge off the hook, assuming a premature 'down the pub' celebration. Yet this was a disease whose end could not, with any finality, ever be celebrated.

Within the first two days of radiotherapy the tumour, as predicted, was much reduced. Then, on day three, 'it' came back. I rang the doctors from home and said, 'It's coming back.' There was disbelief.

Ron was readmitted to hospital, this time into isolation. With his immune system fading, another programme of radiotherapy and a new regime of chemo was prescribed. Threatened death needs mindless life as company: Wimbledon balls hit every year in the same way; the Pink Panther and Peter Sellers never died on film. We let go of control, feeling our way through tragedy and fatigue. With the reality of life blown away, we were truly 'alive' for the first time in our lives. If television could keep hold of some normality in Ron's space, then music did in mine. At night when Anna was at the hospital and Luke was asleep, I could cry noise; big sessions to timely anthems of that year – Bruce Springsteen's 'Philadelphia', REM's 'Everybody Hurts', k. d. lang's 'Constant Craving' and Mozart.

The rapid return of the disease had thrown us. Moreover, it had thrown Glazer. We now had his full attention; very few got in. There was always Caroline, and always will be. There were my mother and father, Luke and Anna, Ann, Sophie, Liz and José. On the inner circle, that was all I could cope with. People grow uncomfortable at the idea of death at such a young age. Somewhere around us, Ron's illness was sparking off so many reactions in others. It had marked a spot where others could afford to ask why they did what they did and with whom. He liberated, through the threat to his own mortality, a freedom for others to debate theirs.

The period during which he was most ill alienated as many people and friends as it attracted. Some simply could not speak to me: some had cures in mind; some tried so hard, they prayed, chanted and dreamed of his return to

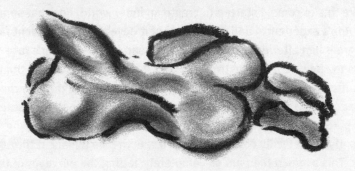

MR Brinker sleeping

Animated Version OF MR Brinkers.

Luke's doodles of his dad,
drawn in Charing
Cross Hospital

health. At the height of this collective well-wishing, the doctors discovered that his lungs, spleen and kidneys were showing shades of cancer and there was only one more chance. They called it the Big Bang.

Screaming, crying, moaning, farting, vomiting, with snot the size of full-grown locusts – there is little a body can do to shock or revolt. After a while, you become enmeshed in pursuing the goal; bodily shame no longer matters. On the afternoon that, totally constipated and in agony, Ron cried out as a nurse physically had to pull it out of him, there was no possible return to romance, to games, to flirting or to sex. Just a hell-for-leather drive to live. What might shock the outside circle wasn't worth the trouble to explain. I raged at those whose lives just bumbled along, who hadn't seen what I had seen. I had become a 'death snob': wiser than you, normal life impossible. I was facing something inside, triggered by Ron. He never thought he would die. Shamefully, I thought he was going to. I became harder and harder to touch.

My death-snob syndrome became exclusive. In no order of preference, the following were banned:

1 OTHER PEOPLE'S GURUS IN MY FACE.
2 FURTHEST REMOVED RELATIVES, ANCESTORS, COUSINS, WHO HAVE HAD IT AND SURVIVED.
3 OBSERVATIONS ON HIS STATE OF MIND.
4 TOUCHING LUKE.
5 LOVE DIRECTED AT ME.
6 BEING HAPPY IN MY PRESENCE.
7 ADMITTING THAT YOU HAVE PROBLEMS THAT CAN RIVAL THIS.

You couldn't touch me, except inside-out.

But I had a friend on the inside: Dr Ed Kanfer. He was the chief of Big Bangs and he spoke to me as I wanted to be spoken to. He had seen eyes that had said goodbye to the outside world, carers who balanced hospital life with all roads home. I liked him then and I like him now. Of chances, he spoke with an exceptional bluntness; of what was to come – the smell of it; the future, the risk of it; and life – 'It'll never be the same again.' He was in charge of the Bone Marrow Unit.

The BMU is a club. BMU kids and their families shared the communal kitchen with the bad-tempered but harmlessly humming cleaner. The routine allows for a strange sense of safety in a process which was described by Ed as throwing a hand-grenade into a body and hoping for the best. At first, getting Ron booked into this club wasn't easy, but a new professor from whom Glazer took advice managed to schedule him in and on 24 August 1993 he entered the unit.

Barbara was Ron's first BMU nurse. She had the skill of that first pair of professional hands that picked up Luke as soon as he was born: so much smiling confidence and obvious ability that the recipient can perhaps feel that the process of birth, or in this case the sustaining of life, can be a relaxing affair.

Kate Dodd, nicknamed by Luke the 'Dude', saved lives seemingly with a smile and made pain almost acceptable. With her Ron inhabited that temporary zone in which he was neither certain to live nor destined to die.

Before the Big Bang could begin, bone marrow had to be removed. This process is known as 'harvesting' and in Ron's case, as his own marrow was to be given back to him through a transplant later on, it was known as an autograft. Both marrow and bone would have to be removed in order to establish that it was free of lymphoma. For those in the business of curing there is habit; for the first-time receivers there is fear. The closeness of the two can produce a unique humour. Ron asked me to stay with him while they anaesthetized the lower part of his back. I sat down facing him as he lay on his side. As important as ever was to show no measure of my own fear or react to what was being done. This is perhaps the most exhausting part of being the other, keeping things normal in a situation that is not.

Outside the room the young receptionist sat chatting on the phone. She had an East End accent mixed up with the elongated and disapproving vowels of a gossipy woman. Ron had had bone marrow removed twice before but I had not been present. The marrow was easily extricated; it is in fact a type of bloody fluid. Harder to remove is the bone. Ron's eyes shut on the impact as the doctor dug a wide needle into the back of his pelvis. I think of the needles used for this harvest process as more like lino-cutting tools. I began to sweat into Ron's hand as they tugged in a circular motion at the bone in his back.

A just audible conversation went on outside. 'Oh, don't. You're so wicked – stop it!'

And as the words 'you frisky thing' came through the door, the lino-cutting tool dug further into Ron's back. Due to the hardness of Ron's bones, it was necessary to bounce him up and down on the end of the needle. With great strength, the doctor tugged out the piece of bone.

'I'll see you on Wednesday, you *wicked* thing!'

Everybody has to find their own way with an illness like this. It was Ron's father who introduced Ron to a Dutch doctor – a doctor whom Ron did not meet throughout his illness. He managed to hold Ron in a place where, he believed, he would live if he hung on. Dr Egon Massink works from Hilversum in Holland. A spiritual healer, he tells you your chances at the onset. Ron's father provided him with a black-and-white photo of Ron aged nine and from this he said he was able to picture his brain pattern and his spiritual blue-print. He worked, primarily, through telepathy, a form of energy transference. I firmly believe now that there are parts of ourselves that are accessible only through trauma and shock. With distance it may be called wisdom, but at the time it is an openness to self only the sight of the end can trigger. Ron spoke to Massink often, sometimes during the day, sometimes at night, and occasionally he faxed him.

With this sort of disease, temperature is the simplest indicator of either infection or spread, and when antibiotics make no difference you know that 'it' is on the move again. One evening, while I was sitting in his room, trying to gauge how he felt while chatting normally about the outside world, his temperature shot up to over forty degrees and the shivering started. His black woollen hat was pulled down as low as possible. Barely visible, Ron lay wrapped in blankets. Glasses held a wad of cotton-wool to his eye. It had been a one-way journey so far and neither of us had looked back yet to take on board what had happened.

The room was an identikit space for pumping fluids through bodies. Everything in it lent itself to the purpose of infusion and flushing. We were both attached to it – Ron literally and me emotionally. He described to me that he was hallucinating: a row of giant Negroes in suits were walking towards him and through him. They came processionally through the wall, passed through his body and out into the room beyond.

Like blinking, there came a time when Ron's presence disappeared and reappeared before me – just gone for a moment, during which, perhaps, I didn't know the person, the treatment or the disease. As an animal twitching in death, this was how my mind coped with my belief that I was watching him die. My father had the gift to sit with him, and 'it', and did so every day, often in the afternoons, in silence. He was the only one (apart from, perhaps, his mother) whom Ron felt he could sleep in front of and didn't have to report anything to, didn't have to respond to the 'you'll make it' brigade.

The most restorative periods for Ron were the silent ones, and only those capable of doing it mattered to me. My version of Dad's time with him was to draw. I drew him sleeping, and I designed a collection. Having a pen in my hand made me feel normal, but I couldn't relate to the fabrics, I couldn't feel them, and in feeling nothing for them I was aware how numb I was. The barometer of my feelings was registered through a lack of spontaneity to cloth. This had never happened before. I was becoming bereft of the very thing that had recently defined me.

Ron's temperature went up further and my newly acquired experience told me we were at a dangerous stage. I urged him to call Massink, which he did. Massink answered straight away. Afterwards, I thought that he had been waiting for the call. They talked briefly. In his understated way, Ron said he wasn't feeling good. I think Massink could tell from his voice and from the level of his treatment that Ron was low. Ron put the phone down and within minutes described sensations in his head, things he hadn't felt before, an alarming sense of increased heat. Twenty-five minutes later his temperature was as low as mine.

Where Ron did express great anxiety was concerning any kind of pain, and I think that the moment his illness acquired an official stamp for him was the implanting of the Hickman line. For me, it was also a great barrier to cross. The Hickman line is essential for a Big Bang to take place, because the sheer volume of fluid and the number of tubes necessary to complete it cannot be held in the veins. It is a four-wire tube: the central tube passes through the skin and chest and dips into the top of the heart; the three tubes outside are for the intake of fluids and drugs. One tube would take TPN (total parental nutrition). By this stage Ron could no longer eat; his throat was raw from radiotherapy and his tongue and mouth ulcerated. The second and third tubes took the bags of individual drugs which made up a process called the protocol. Ron's treatment was known as the lace protocol and it would take seven days to administer.

I learned how to flush the Hickman line. This was as scary to do as was the thought that it was the first new thing I'd learned in ten years – a decade of doing what I loved, stumbling and fumbling with obstacles on the way but essentially believing I could do the bit that really mattered, design. Flushing the line involved incredible hygiene, trust, probably not that much skill but a sense of both priority and order. Fear of injecting a splinter of glass from a broken phial into the top of Ron's heart was my main preoccupation. And the secondary one, which I never overcame, was the withdrawal of blood backwards out of the heart, to make sure I was in the right tube.

During this period I had a dream. I dreamed I had a second child made of glass, perfect in every detail. It was born in a position that would allow it to stand, lie or sit. I took it to a family gathering, so they could meet it for the first time. I sat it on the end of the mantelpiece and, as I expected, it fell off, smashing into pieces on the ground. The baby also knew that it would fall. My father left the room to write something to me, something I feared greatly, and my uncle shouted for someone to confront me with my crime. I then left the room to go to the basement, a huge place only partly decorated by me but well on the way to becoming something special. I packed a bag only slightly heavier than I could carry with ease, and left. I dreamed out the rest of my life in varying ages, engaged in eternally repeating escape scenes, the first in Dickensian times, fleeing with the help of a cloaked man who let me hide in his horse-drawn carriage. And in France I escaped arrest in 1971, when I was spotted outside a sixties purpose-built hospital but not caught. I ran through the past, present and future, always in the same clothes, unable to disguise myself to the time I was in. The future approached. Still a fugitive, I was now infamous for the killing of my baby. I was awoken outside by the bang of a dustman.

During this time, despite everything, there were moments of laughter, spiced presumably by the foreign nature of it all. Throughout the Big Bang we sustained attempts at cleanliness. On day six of the protocol, almost fully poisoned by the series of drugs, Ron decided to have a shower. He was by now similar in appearance to the famous photograph of a Bosnian man behind chicken-wire in Yugoslavia. It took half an hour to move him – wire, drips, pumps – into the tiny shower room. Undressing him was always silently alarming because he was so thin. As I pulled down his pyjamas to a feather-less, bird-like frame, I had to make an effort not to reveal my true feelings: his emaciated state, so inexplicably desirable in my industry, so wretched and distressing in this one.

Clothes removed, head ducked – he was too tall for the unit – water on, soap-up time. This too was slow, so as not to jog the Hickman wound or the bandages on his eye. The soaping was going well – in fact, full coverage had been achieved. Pleased with our progress, we watched in disbelief as the water cut out. We froze. I stared at him, lathered like a leek; he stared back at me, replaying the effort it had taken to get into the fucking thing in the first place. Flannel and soap cemented in my hands, I broke up. After all we were going through, it didn't seem possible that Thames Water could inflict this ultimate humiliation. My laughter was hysterical. I cried, my belly ached, and I wet myself. We ran the film in reverse and I put Ron, no more than mildly disgruntled, back to bed. He seemed pleased to hear me laugh but bewildered by its intensity. He settled in, the long trip over, and buzzed the nurse to change one of the chemo bags.

The back view of my father has always provoked sadness in me. I can remember the sequence of back views from my childhood to this day – in part physical – the slightly rounded upper back with leftover powerful shoulders, stooped, I imagine, like his father, who spent his life as a miner. I finally made sense of it one day when, in partnership with Ron, two back views walked away from me down the hospital corridor to radiotherapy. Ron in his purple BHS dressing-gown walked slowly by my father's side. Theirs was a connected stroll, as at home in illness as it was in health. There was neither physical support needed, as the pace was slow, nor verbal communication, as the place they were going to was by now routine. They were, at that moment, the same. Ron's illness and closeness to death made sense of a part of my father's spirit: one facing it, the other recognizing it. They were a couple, joined together by something I could not share.

It was a relief for a moment to witness the long unsaid so visually. I have a photograph of me being held by my dad when I was about one: it was taken slightly from below and so is framed quite timelessly by sky. With eyes that I imagine couldn't focus properly, he and I are both locked on to an identical view. The photograph suggests that this is something some distance away and in my darkest moments it has kept me brave and special, feeling that there is the possibility that we were destined to see the same things, whatever the landscape, no matter where we are.

I watched them together on many occasions, often only a glimpse when I came into the room to do an afternoon shift. There would always be a moment to observe them both together: Dad in the chair in the corner wearing the unisex and incongruous white plastic apron that protected no one from anything – he looked vaguely ridiculous, as we all did – and Ron, sometimes sleeping on top of the covers, suspended from drips and pumps, and at other times completely submerged under blankets and his black woolly hat. These times represent for me the most special moments between my father and myself, the experience made unique by Ron's relentless journey.

Once in radiotherapy, we had to let go of Ron as he disappeared round the corner to face the part he did on his own. Towards the end of the treatment – perhaps it was the last day – I asked if I could go round the corner, down the short corridor to where all the months of action had taken place – the space Ron knew so well. I was surprised by the size of the room. It was big, the placing of the table in the middle with nothing around it a sign of the distance healthy people had to keep from the treatment of the ill. Most frightening of all were the straps, of which I had been unaware. Ron's clear plastic mask, made at the start of his treatment, was marked with coloured felt-pen across the face to indicate the route rays of varying intensity would take. The right side had large geometric holes cut in, outlining the area they had to hit.

On realizing they strapped his head to the table, I felt guilty I had not taken this on board; hadn't shared this missing bit and so had somehow let him down. Ron's illness was his, but at times I wished it was infectious. At one point, I even had his doctors doing some of the more mundane tests on me. I developed pains in my heart and went to have them checked. Stress was diagnosed. Dad, Luke and I had our pulses and blood-pressures taken one day, partly in an effort to make the simpler things look normal for Luke, and partly also because I couldn't believe it was possible for us to go through our side of all this without some physical side-effects.

It almost slipped by us one day. Keeping Luke entertained during hospital visits was difficult; he hated the smell, the communal TV room dotted with people who looked as if they would not make it and who, perhaps more importantly to Luke, didn't like *Neighbours*. Luke made everything normal, his response to things – 'yuk' – welcome. Very occasional tears – invariably triggered by mine – made even the most painful thoughts thinkable.

One afternoon he quietly picked up some wax crayons next to Ron's bed, together with a pack of blank white postcards. We had often encouraged him to draw to fill up the time. Neither of us paid particular attention. Calmly, he drew one incredible image after another. The directness and symbolism could only have come through a child's hand. His peaceful industry continued until, twelve miniature paintings later, he ran out of postcards.

A strange moment arrives when you see the unforeseeable for the first time. You look to find a common understanding on the face of others; you search for anything familiar – you need to position it next to something else just to be able to swallow. The relevance and profligacy of his drawings made me almost uneasy in his presence. A message from a little man: 'I love you to infinity and back and no return.' He had caught the colour of cancer; he had given the disease a face. The enemy I had identified all those months ago became acceptable in Luke's hands. Pinned to the noticeboard for the duration of the treatment, they always drew comment, as passive and by-the-way as when they had first been drawn.

The diary entry for 31 August looks like this: white blood count 0.1, haemoglobin 9.6, platelets 67. On the wall a white drawing board was kept to record the rise and fall of the white blood count either side of the Big Bang, and although still confined to his isolation room, Ron had had a busy day. The eye doctor came, then he had a chest X-ray, ECG heart scan, stitches taken out of his Hickman wound, placed on a heart monitor, antibiotic drips, three blood transfusions, aromatherapy, anti-sickness drips, TPN drips and, I wrote in my diary, 'a million pills'. Late the same day his bone marrow was transfused back. The smell of sweet and sickly sweetcorn filled the room, an odour that made me retch. It had to be tolerated by all of us as part of the transplant process.

We were awaiting the vital days ahead to see if Ron's system would come back to life again. On the whole, we were successful at always having one of the A-team with him. Above all, he never wanted to be alone. On one of the nights – and for some reason I've made no record of it in my diary – I was on my way home alone at midnight. I had called a cab from the firm we had been using, to ferry the only member of my family who couldn't drive at the time, me, back to north London. I stood outside the hospital door for around fifteen minutes. Wearily, I was about to call them, when a man stuck his head out of a car. It was dark. I couldn't see very clearly and frankly was too knackered. He said my name and that the cab was held up and asked if I would like to check it on his radio. I didn't and, completely out of character for me, at his suggestion, got into the back of his. He knew where I was going. He asked if there was anyone special that I'd been visiting and I told him yes. He replied that he had once had a tumour in his head ('protruding out the back like a grapefruit') and that Professor Newlands had treated it – coincidentally, the same doctor as Ron's. As he told his story, which included a flight to India to meet a spiritual healer and a dietitian, I watched his eyes in the mirror, which he had adjusted to examine mine. He told me Ron was going to be okay. As ever, this felt insulting. Many a conversation with the ferrymen of that period ran along the same concerned yet useless lines.

When we reached my road he pulled over and looked at me through the gap in the headrest. Once again, only his eyes were visible. I offered to pay him but he continued talking, telling me how this was his last night on the job and I was his last passenger. He was going to KL in Malaysia the next day. This is where Ron's parents live. He refused the money, saying that the trip didn't need to be paid for.

Next morning it all seemed odd. I told my story to Caroline, who out of curiosity called the cab company. There was no record of a request for a pick-up that night and no driver had been available at that time. As far as they knew, the driver didn't exist. When I went back to the hospital the next day, Ron's white blood count was lifting.

The white count had to rise above 3.0 before Ron could be considered well enough to go home. Meanwhile, the foundations under the house in which we had a flat had been moving and – along with them – the walls. At no weeks' notice I had to find us somewhere to live and finish the collection. Anna continued doing everything she could to keep us going, as did my mother and father. My mother had taken Luke away for the week of the Big Bang – I didn't want him to see Ron, or myself, during this time. Until now Luke had learned about and followed a lot of what Ron was going through, but the hand-grenade description had prompted me to send him away – somewhere sunny, busy and loving.

Getting to grips with all the things I had always left to Ron was unwelcome – building insurance policies, a peculiar and somewhat shifty relationship with the freeholder and irate but very helpful neighbours – and, inevitably, very badly timed. I finally found a flat to rent in Fitzjohns Avenue. We were covered by the house insurance, and Anna and I cleared our possessions, moving everything upstairs to the floor where all this had started five months before.

Granusite Colony Stimulant Factor (GCSF) is a well-known drug used to encourage white cell count recovery, and along with numerous blood transfusions and antibiotics this was the treatment for the next few weeks. Three days into the mandatory eighteen required for 'recovery', Ron mysteriously developed a suntan, a bizarre moment for skin colour to return. Nurses and doctors alike found it very amusing, as did I. With his tan came a rise in spirits, a relief that his organs were coming out of shock and that the heavy drugs were over.

I had a post-treatment meeting with Kanfer in the drugs cupboard, sitting on boxes of bandages and cans of medical-looking liquid. We talked of chances. He said he'd been pleased with Ron's progress but that the positive response to his coming out of Big Bang bore no link to remission. His chances remained, after all this, at the very best 50/50.

At work I received a call from Ron to say his blood count had leapt to 1.3 – unheard of during treatment such as his. I immediately called Dad, good and bad news never being completely digestible without his response. When, jubilantly, I went to visit later, I found Ron crushed. It was somebody else's count. Ron's was still at 0.1.

It's odd how some news will gut you and other news doesn't. I can remember an incredible calm when Professor Newlands told us that he had found shadows throughout Ron's body. In fact, I had been out of the room. The repeating of the news had made it a by-the-way statement. The blood count mistake had all of us on the floor for quite a while. And the healthy tan disappeared as quickly as it had come, courtesy of a drug which reversed the deceptiveness of its presence.

It was a strange target to reach for, leaving a room. There was no moment of completion, no finishing line, no certainty that it had gone – just the relief that the process to blow it away hadn't take Ron with it. Ron continued to contact Massink and take some herbal drugs that he had been sending over. He also took some giant pills somewhat flippantly called life extension formula!

On the day that Ron was told he could leave, packing his possessions became both a difficult and a moving experience. We didn't want to leave: a fear of leaving the lifeline, going back to the world and to a strange flat – it was all too sudden. Packing took ages. I didn't want them to wipe the blood count off the board. I didn't want another young man or woman to enter this bed and go through what we had. There was little sight of our doctors until quite late on. The word spread down to radiotherapy that Ron was about to be discharged. Glazer came up. It had been a while since we had come out of his intensive care and into Kanfer's hands. 'I don't want to see you for ten years,' he said cheerfully. I didn't know whether that was good or bad. He had a good feeling about Ron and didn't think that we would meet again.

Ed came to say goodbye, entering the room as a friendly chum might a pub. I always wondered what he made of our relationship, that he could tell me things and not Ron. Experience, I guess, had made him accurate about the separate journeys taken by the ill and the carer. He gave congratulations and warnings to Ron, and the prospect of hope to me.

Caryn Franklin had given me a silver heart on a leather thong. It held lavender incense. She gave it to me when we met briefly on one of the surreal occasions when I had trooped off back into the world of health. Whenever I was about to become overwhelmed, I opened the top and breathed long and deep. A new and welcome weight around my neck tapped the care of others into my chest when I most needed it.

On the day of discharge, none of us was ready. When it came to it, we sensed Ron needed to linger. Ron paced a bit and wafted us towards the door. Now dressed, he was someone else. His Levi's huge and belted, his pre-illness uniform didn't suit him any more. We waited by the lift. As it opened, a couple I recognized from months before came out. The woman was tired but full of habit and order, the man in his wheelchair, at a guess, back from radiotherapy. She looked down at our bags, knowing me but not the new situation. With more laps to go herself, she could not bring herself to say goodbye.

Minutes later I went back to check on Ron. He was still in the room, negotiating the wrench. We looked at each other and in silence I left. Through the doors of the hospital to the outside, the bed habits that had once held our full attention were lost to the newness of walking and meeting oncoming traffic. 'It's all so green,' were Ron's comments on greeting the air.

What is the attraction to a place one has survived? The word 'remission' does not allow a bare arse to its brickwork. I have detoured cabs to go past the hospital. I have stood in front of the building looking up at his window – weeping, angry and grateful. When passing on a riverboat months later, on a brighter day, it sent its stench into the air and the rest of the journey. I wasn't ill and I wasn't treated. I felt no physical pain. I slept in my own bed every night, yet a part of me was threatened all the same.

Back in our pink-walled flat in Fitzjohns Avenue with a pool full of leaves outside, we pretended to accept our new condition. I was over a stone heavier from Anna's wonderful cooking and Ron was starting to eat again.

In early October I went to visit the collection that had taken shape over the phone and by fax and had been put together by a number of remarkable people. I designed the first scratchings of the Spring/Summer 1994 collection, sitting next to Ron on a stool in a communal chemo ward. The collection was called *Providence*.

I had a need to protect myself by scribbling. Sitting in this room among the wigged and headscarfed people, sharing the disease and their treatment openly, made it somehow harder to fight. It brought home to us that we were only one of thousands. What could Ron bring to battle against it that none of these people hadn't? What, beyond treatment, ultimately determined who survived and who died?

There's no escaping the commonplace of cancer, particularly when there are ten people linked up to drips. A cowshed at milking time – though I've never seen one – might have had the same relaxed and inevitable routine: smiles and efficiency and much patience to hand as the chemo took five hours to drip through.

I couldn't draw women, I could draw only straight lines: shirts, trousers and dresses – no bodies. My usual process to design had been to draw the woman first. She came out of my pen and told me what to do, who she was, what she wanted. When the dreaming has gone too far, I am halted by the instruction of what a woman might want to pay for it.

It was important to carry on, partly because there was a business which people depended on for their livelihoods – one which Caroline was supporting under enormous pressure. I needed it for far more selfish reasons. At the time I was my work; I was 'Helen Storey'. I relied on her to remind me of what was real and what wasn't. In private I saw my name detach itself and set sail for another season without me aboard.

The collection was being shown in a private house in Knightsbridge and I arrived to a hubbub of activity in a room of familiar faces. Despite having gone into work most mornings during this period, to see the clothes on the rails for the first time was strange. Decisions had had to be made in my absence. I saw glimpses of where I had started boldly before the illness, finished off with sense and precision, no roughness or broken edge.

That the collection existed at all was down to two people. I had been work-ing with Mark for a number of years. He claims that I'm really a painter and I that he is really a sculptor. The homelessness of these qualities in our industry is what gives us an edge over those who are motivated by profit alone. If I drew a line, he knew where my hand would go and where it would stop. He would get inside my vision and, protecting his own version of it, bully to the end to make it real. Many a time his skill as a pattern-maker and his ability to visualize the feel of a collection have been the only things to keep me at it. If you go back to the best work of most key British designers, you'll probably find that Mark was employed by most of them. He is the quiet and loud effector.

The second person had the hardest task of all, employed in my absence by Caroline to be my eyes and ears on a collection by someone she barely knew. Debo was a positive spirit. She ordered my day and my brain. I turned up to sprint through the impossible before going to the hospital late every morning, asking her the same questions four times, forgetting the answers and expect-ing too much. At times she must have wondered why we were attempting this at all. We met in strange circumstances, and parted in them too.

I sat at the back of the room, talking occasionally to buyers and press, ashamed of the effort that the collection had involved, jealous of those whose creative lives had gone on undisturbed and unable to impart a grain of how I really felt.

Ron was back at the flat. He slept till eleven or twelve every day, his rela-tionship with his mother immensely strong. Food was the stuff of his childhood – Dutch chocolate bits on bread. He travelled backwards and forwards to the hospital for check-ups and then the big spaces came. Four-week blocks of 'no need to see you'. A barren time of not knowing, of mistaking swollen morning eyes for tumour, of fear at the slightest rise in temperature – it's back.

Ron had cried twice. Once because of the needles: formidable in number, due to the amount of the drugs, it was hard to believe that they involved a plan of action. And the other time was when his mother and I came into the room unusually late one morning. Sitting on the edge of the bed, his back to us, he was trying to do something for himself. Forcing down substitute food, he turned around and saw us in the same frame. He burst out crying. His mother hung back for me to go forward. He dropped his spoon. His wound of a sob was without rhythm and throaty. Our gossipy, sisters of care entrance – made imperative by the relentless need for us to be there – had reduced him to tears a second time.

Drawing from Ron's sketch book, Rome, 1984

There is a detached part of Ron, somewhere he goes or is where I am not. It has always been there. In my angry moments, it is an intolerable deafness. In the aftermath, it is the part of his spirit not to be shared, a serenity I can only envy. I have provoked it to battle; nothing has happened. I have ignored it, for long periods, to my own cost. But if I remain true to this period of our lives, it stands as the part that allowed him to heal himself. To think I could bring something to this process was foolish; the power that I wielded in my work and 'art' useless.

Slow-pedalling away from our recent hell, from a distance, I am changed, he more so himself. There is now an insistence in me that life must have a vitality that only the threat of its end can bring, an acknowledgement that in our lives there is only the undesigned.

Postscript: three years on Ron is still in remission and would like to thank the following people: Helen, Luke, Mum, Dad, Daniel, Barbara, Caroline, everyone at the Charing Cross and Egon. Thank you for my life.

This chapter is dedicated to the Imperial Cancer Research Fund and to all those affected by cancer.

11

Edith's

Sisters

I have to thank the fashion press. They have supported me rigorously through-out my ten years. They record and travel parallel to all that we as designers do. They translate and make clearer the vision that is ours to a public that is theirs. In designing the only way I know how, I have been an erratic talent to follow. In being on the whole a private person, I have not aided the process by networking. In short, there has been at times both an abundance to report and a lost muddle to decipher. We have a long-distance yet intimate relation-ship. The writing up of shows has in the past been important for a sense of self-worth, especially for the designers who put their clothes forward as pro-jections of their personalities as much as commodities. We remain hypersen-sitive to the individual reaction of a few key members of the press. Did any of them leave before the end of the show? Did their pens move much? Did they chat through it? Did they wear dark glasses, the ultimate insult to any design-er with a love of colour?

It is both hard and scary to court an honest opinion from the press. So much the better then to overhear it unsolicited from a journalistic giant. Attending a Clarence House reception in aid of the fashion industry hosted by HRH The Princess of Wales, I was sitting on the toilet, engulfed by fake fur and velvet from the current collection, my hand precariously balanced on the flush, when I overheard a familiar splutter asking of the great and good lady at the next sink, 'Tho what do you think of Helen Thtorey, eh, eh, eh?' I sat rigid on my seat, a once in a lifetime chance to hear where I ranked. The response was, 'I think she's one of the most interesting ones we've got.' The grateful hack said she agreed, logged it somewhere in her collection of opin-ions and left. I waited a few minutes for the coast to clear, before ascending the palatial stairs to enjoy being told at the top, what an interesting designer I was from the same spluttering lips.

On the whole, I am a stronger Autumn/Winter designer. My mistake in sum-mer has always been to imagine that we have one. Retail sales and mark-ups are so out of sync with our real seasons, in terms of weather, that it is unusu-al for a designer to make vast amounts of money during this period. In England, if you want a swimsuit, the best time to buy it is when it's cold, in February or March, and in August, when it's more than likely to be hot, you can find yourself a 'nice' woollen overcoat. I have never understood why this ridiculous pattern of ignoring our climate has gone unchallenged for so long. We should today be working towards a seasonless year with drops of ranges throughout to commercially cushion the environmental and economic changes which surround us. This is not an easy concept for young designers; smaller ranges, less volume, mean far more risk on their part.

Good Inside,
1994

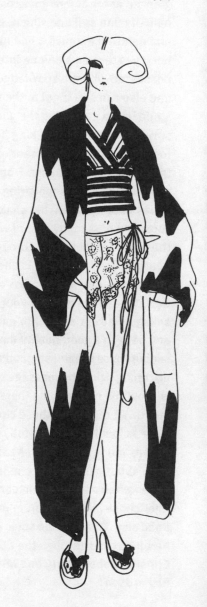

One of my stronger Autumn/Winter collections was called *Rebecca*, after a childhood friend I no longer know. Autumn/Winter 1994 was the first show since Ron had been ill and, having missed the Spring/Summer in terms of a 'show' the season before, I was keen to feel the blood flow again. I had used many of our most commercial fabrics and shapes but also experimented at the other end with my Planet de Voire velvet – my painting for the year, an expensive vision of the universe which, despite its huge price, was as commercially successful in terms of margins as our stretch-satin jeans.

There is a model called Susie Bick who is adored by many a designer. Rare within her profession, she can become someone new every time without dissipating her own self. Occasionally, a design comes out, seemingly unconscious of the fact that it makes little sense with the rest of the collection. It sits on the page and insists that it is made up. In *Rebecca*, Susie wore one such design. Sent out on the catwalk alone, she was wearing a black velvet bias-cut coat with raven black and oil-green feathers curving up to hide her face. The tail of the coat was devilish and snaked thin to a point six feet behind her.

Her eyes went red in the flash of the camera lights and she held a crook of a stick as tall as herself. I left behind the voices of the buyers: 'Who the hell would wear that?' 'Can't see myself running for a bus or eating soup in it.' She was there for me alone. She glanced at me before going on, passing a pain of mine as if knowing it. In her innocent and death-like stance, I had nearly known her. Eyes take on a unique intensity when possessed with the knowledge of another no one else can see; a girl in the wings, she stood in the gap facing the audience and stayed there waiting. Taking her first step forward in that thin moment of divide, she took all my pain with her. From behind my screen, my gaze disappearing into black velvet as tired eyes can, her snaking tail gave a consciousness to my love of what I do. Of all the priorities that faded through the threat of death in Ron's illness, this one had not.

As important as the press are the 'celebrities'. Celebrities wearing your clothes can be as big an advertisement or endorsement as any page in a good quality magazine. I love seeing these women so good at what they do, recognizing the message on the hanger without me having to be there or open my mouth. At their best, these clothes have sung as loudly and powerfully as they, have said as much about them as silently they have about me. Michael and Janet Jackson wore *Rebecca* for their 'Scream' video and Cher chose pieces of it from our King's Road shop. That season some of my other heroines came through the door: Julie Christie, Debbie Harry and Miranda Richardson.

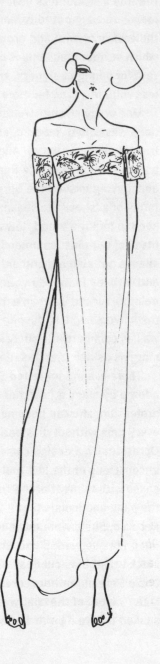

Good Inside, 1994

A black limousine larger than the shop front blocked the light to guide Cher through the front door. Whenever a 'somebody' special came in, usually American, we would shut the shop for them. On this day I was hiding up on the landing at the back and could hear her walking around and clunking hangers. Music was playing in the shop and, slowly and very naturally, she started to sing – through the clothes and her voice, a private and intimate concert to me behind the curtain, shy as ever. Caroline encouraged me to go and introduce myself. Cher had been buying my clothes consistently for six years in the States and this was the first time she had come to London to buy them. I walked up to her and past, hoping she would somehow sense the connection. She was still singing, by now quite emotionally, and I had to turn back again and introduce myself. She was warm and was used to humble and embarrassed approaches. It took the girls in the shop weeks to tell me that, having met me, Cher had two things to say about me: wasn't she sweet, and she's got my old teeth!

The Spring/Summer collection, called *Good Inside,* marked our tenth anniversary which we celebrated by producing a magazine, edited by Sally Brampton and art-directed by John Hind. I had long looked forward to a time when I could work with Sally. I had met her once at the beginning of my career when she worked at the *Observer* and I recall abbreviating her name to Sal two minutes into our conversation – an unwelcome familiarity at the time. Some of the silliest moments have prompted my climb,

Good Inside, 1994

Edith's Sisters, 1995

not least of all to reach the day when Sally would welcome me shortening her name.

A collection with an idea that technology had not yet made possible, lavender had been with me during 1993–4 and I wanted to develop a cloth which could capture that scent. I wanted to stretch fabric into the realms of aura. Beyond what cashmere makes you feel or the attitude which rubber demands, it was an experiment with cloth and scent together. Trapping wild lavender under silk organza in panels, hems, inside collars and into removable hearts on T-shirts was where I landed up. I ascertained it could be cleaned and that the scent remained. I offered alternative fragrances as if colour-ways on the same theme. Throughout my career as a fashion designer, what I have failed to secure but desperately wanted was a speedy way to negotiate and swap technology across the industries. I am a designer of ideas; I need the world of science as much as I ever did the textile industry. With only six months, and sometimes less, between the seasons, instincts are hard to pursue. R&D remains dreamed and doodled so that black dresses and those satin jeans can sell. To control the energy found in static, to *ombre* fabric through its gauge and density and not just its colour, to spray cloth on to the body, to pursue my wandering mind to its Lycra limits, these were always constant frustrations for me.

Once again, the catwalk was not the place to waft a new idea across and the collection on the whole was unbalanced, as other parts of it struggled to visually make

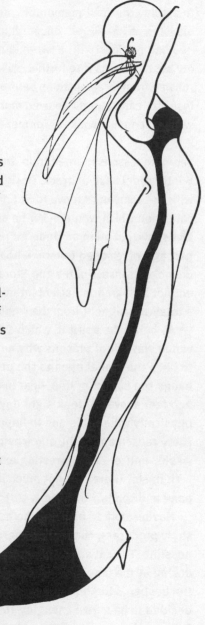

Edith's Sisters, 1995

up for the subtlety of the original concept. It is at times like these that I have often wondered about the perils of the catwalk. By designing for it as a specific medium, much more gentle or genuine ideas get lost and are often, therefore, not pursued. It was also a collection at the finale of which I chose to display the most memorable pieces from my previous ten years. It was a disaster, as knackered, uncoordinated pieces trooped out on models whom I had had no time to fit: a two-minute botched job of a funeral in homage to all my best ideas. As if to further cock it up, a model who hadn't made it to the runway from three sections before wandered out, amidst the retrospective, a lost lilac cardigan, made even more ridiculous by the determination with which the model walked. For me, *Good Inside* was rotten.

Yet more lessons learned from *Good Inside* saw *Edith's Sisters* (Autumn/ Winter 1995) back on track. Designed in two days and completed, along with the company's move to St Christopher's Place, in seven weeks, it was a collection which would never be produced. Unknown to us, it was to be our last show, put on in an Underground tunnel in South Kensington – the same passage which used to ferry a board four-year-old to the museums. In an unspoken sense, Coates and Storey was on its last legs. This became apparent not by a gradual lack of interest, as one imagines near an end, but rather a total commitment from the whole team to do it as well as we could.

As befits the spirit in which Caroline and I have tackled everything, the venue was full of reasons why not to. The first of these was a requirement to keep the tunnel open to the public until two hours before the show. To gauge the impact of this, bear in mind that tents, the alternative venues, 200 feet above us, took eight days to erect to pull off the same purpose. I physically willed this one to happen, grovelling and scraping, pre-empting every reason under the sun why they wouldn't want to do it. We had three weeks' notice – an interesting exercise in the interpretation of proceeding with haste. There was not much in common between this tiny fashion company and London Transport.

Having worked out who the action men were at LT, Caroline, Liz and our show producers, Nick and Cameron, sat down to work out if it was at all possible. The catwalk was three minutes long. The audience could be dozing by the time outfit number one had returned and the abilities of even the best girls to shine would be stretched. In acknowledgement of this, we decided to have two changing-rooms, one at either end: outfit one at the Science Museum, outfit two at the Natural History. This seemed to work

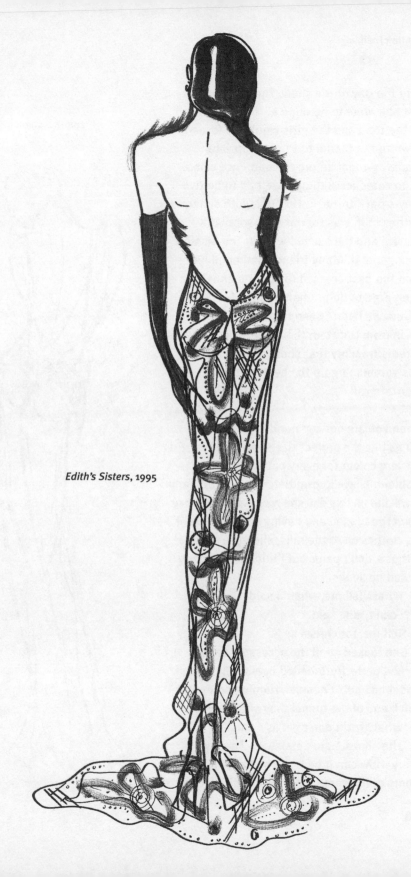

Edith's Sisters, 1995

until the day of the show. The make-up and hair were to be done at the Polish Club up the road and the girls would be ferried down to the tunnel to the appropriate changing-room before the audience came in. To complicate things, we had to do two shows back-to-back. The first, with separate clothes in it, was for our sponsors, Alfa Romeo, and the second was for the fashion pack general. Many friends and employees from the past seemed to spontaneously re-emerge to help: Chantal and Liz Friend, buyers we hadn't seen for years; Gapu and Kevin from Untitled; the model Michelle Paradis from my first show. *Edith's Sisters* was summoning up the best of the past for a curtain call.

Edith's Sisters, 1995

When you are not a major design house, things like the perfect size shoe for every girl in every colour for every outfit can be a problem. I have known Helen Bailey for many years and on this day she was assisting. Once down the tunnel, and having sorted some of the clothes on to the rails, she gave me one of those 'don't panic but I think we've really fucked up' looks.

'What? Tell me, what,' I said.

'I can't,' she said.

'Tell me, for chrissake.'

She looked at all the accessory bags, packed perfectly, labelled beautifully with model and outfit number, running order and which end of the tunnel they should be in.

'What? I still don't get it,' I said.

'The shoes,' she persisted. 'The jewellery. How can it be in both changing-rooms at the same time? She can't just say "excuse me," and leg it down the other end to get them.'

The punch landed.

'Fuck!'

Five-second gap.

'Fuck!'

Another gap.

'Fuck! Quick – split the bags.'

'Split the bags how?' she said calmly.

'Just split them.'

'Can't,' she said. 'We have to work out where each girl will be, in what outfit, at what part of the show, and split everything up into bags that we don't have accordingly.'

With only one hour to go and four models lost, Naomi at the airport with her bag nicked and other assistants, unaware of the mess, drinking vodka at the Polish Club, I panicked. I couldn't think how to bring any order to what we had to do. Someone stuck their head round the cordoned-off end of the tunnel where we were and cheerfully said, 'The tunnel's flooding.'

Rather hurt at my reply, they disappeared. The tunnel was dry when we started the show.

Only a matter of seconds later, another head came through.

'Naomi can't get here.'

This I just ignored. I threw a look like vomit at Nick. He covered his face with a running order for the third time and I told him to go away quietly, find a corner and change it yet again.

'Don't even ask,' I said. 'Just do what you think is best.'

As he left the space, pulling back the curtain with a great whoosh of anxiety, a giant and overwhelming stink of urine came blowing in. Bailey and I looked at each other.

'Susie Menkes,' she said. 'You can just see it, can't you?'

Someone was sent out to replace the water that had no doubt been sucked up by another somebody to spray away the stench.

Bailey finally realized I had reached my end and she became an angel. She threw her halo like a Frisbee the length of the tunnel. She told me to go to the Polish Club and get some vodka down me, which I did. When I returned, as mother she smiled, my little world back in order.

I stroked the clothes, each one hanging where they should be, tapped the odd heel to sit next to its patent partner, and waited. Looking down at myself, having not been aware of what I looked like for the last forty-eight hours,

I realized, grubby in jeans with no socks and a T-shirt, I had to do something about it. I disappeared into a corner and came out in velvet.

The Alfa show went well and even changing the outfits back round the other way for the next one went remarkably smoothly. However, unknown to me backstage, our puddle of rising water had blown the lights at the Natural History end. A gentleman from London Transport grabbed a plate-sized torch, stood on a chair and, shutting his eyes, flashed it on to the bare backside of a model. Mark had watched the first show and came directly towards me.

'Well?' I desperately pleaded, 'Well, what was it like?'

'Needs work,' he said gruffly.

'Needs work?' I repeated, with only half an hour between this one and the next. 'What work?'

'Get Nicholas and Cameron,' he demanded.

I attempted to diffuse the 'fuck-you's' that were about to follow this masculine solution, but in the event the argument was completely wasted as it was over models, one of whom had since gone home with period pains and the other wasn't going to turn up at all.

You can cope with two models not showing up or dropping out, but four is a major disaster. Things got so bad that the team backstage, none of us model potential, swapped silent stares, each looking to see if they believed the other could pull it off. We all agreed none of us could. But out of the audience stepped a model who had watched the last show. She duly agreed at ten minutes' notice to be three people at once.

From time to time Mark and I would spark an idea. Cocooned only by a few other opinions, we occasionally came across something that excited us and that, when least expected, would blow others away. I had designed many of the features in the collection over, under and around the bum, not a new concept in itself. Both Mark and Caroline can spot the things I miss just because my ideas spill out without effort. The lace and flesh dress with no back at all was one of those drawings that was a natural conclusion to a string of commercial ones behind it. Stupid and without reason is okay if there are ten others that aren't and have.

My nerves about using it were calmed by Mark's comment, 'Tell them an old queen told you to do it.'

Following the show, the debate on the zone we all share was astonishing. Bums everywhere. In cartoons John Major's crevice was displayed. On the radio Desmond Morris backed up my instinct for them and on TV the breakfast crowd giggled at them.

The last show was close to how it should have been, the right faces back-stage once again. It can never be thought of as perfect or final – in some ways it wasn't even in keeping with the general direction – that would be to admit you have finished. I haven't. Pulled towards the next something, I feel cat-walks are not right any more. The tunnel was on the way to somewhere else, but I have yet to arrive.

12

Robbie
Coltrane

Last night I slept with Robbie Coltrane. I've been sleeping with him on a regular basis since he became Fitz and I lost my job. Care of him, I have learned how to hover – not fly, but float about ten feet off the ground. The only condition is that I let him hold my feet. I must keep my body streamlined and arms out straight to the sides. He instructs me over the edge and asks me to report back what I can see. Floating over the cliff-face, I tell him of the view, the drop and the sea. He pulls me slowly back into his big arms, his black suit wodgy with affection, my face in his neck. He talks to me close up and knows everything. I want his mind around me for ever.

Time is marked by the next cup of tea and this book. I dream and think a lot nowadays, maybe because I can, because life has slowed to its own riverlike pace and I don't stir it much. Six months ago today our company, Coates and Storey Ltd, went into administrative receivership – into the hands of; we were received. A painful time of contemplation.

Just as with Ron's illness, a few got in and a few were there. Patrick told us what the path ahead would be like, how the team and the world shrinks down to just Caroline and me and how it's the little things that become big. Roger, who had been consistently there for Caroline during that same year, was never far away. Numbness and shock play footy with your self-esteem: we visited a place of no confidence and of complete failure. Through our love for each other, we have taken it in turns to fall to the bottom and come back up again.

Companies go bust all the time and, so I am told, set up shop around the corner the next day. When a business has grown from something as personal as a first thought or an idea, seeing it at any stage as purely corporate, profitable or non-profitable, is quite some step. On the one hand, you are expected to view it as a commodity that either hits the spot or doesn't, and on the other, you *are* the commodity, with life happening to it all the while.

That we hit a three-year string of bad luck is now undeniable, and that we tried to save and pre-empt our financial problems ahead of time is also indisputable. This is for the record. In 1989 Helen Storey Design was a profitable concern. In 1990, as Coates and Storey, we recognized the need for investment to grow. In 1991 we advertised in the *Financial Times* and received eighty responses. Through this particular advert and after much sifting, we secured short-term finance from one key private individual and a smaller amount from another.

In 1992 we expanded into retail and consolidated our wholesale, the Gulf War having affected our order-book significantly. The mechanisms for finding further finance that we tried were as follows: once again we advertised; we worked with investment houses, through the industry, through government schemes and loans; we talked to the DTI; much time-wasting with middle-men; we made direct and targeted approaches; we used the early channels on the Internet and, finally, came close to closing one deal, which fell through on the day of our Spring/Summer 1992 fashion show. We almost went out of business at the end of 1992 when a brand-new fibre which was first proto-typed by us could not be delivered in time to produce finished goods for Autumn/Winter 1993. Sales from this represented 50 per cent of the season's order book and the staggered and late delivery lost us years of buyer confi-dence throughout the world. In order to compensate for the drastic effect of reduced income, we had to fire staff and cut back on all areas to survive. Those staff remaining took pay cuts and Caroline, Ron and I went without salaries for months. Over the years our destiny has been played out as much in the hands of our team as in any luck or lack of it. Underpaid, overworked and bombarded with seasonal chaos, that we lasted as long as we did was as much down to them individually as it ever was to the crazed captains on deck. The frustrations and daily angst were a family affair, the creation of courage perhaps more frequent than any of that softer stuff of mine. The best-selling slogan T shirt of 1992 was 'Shit Happens'.

In 1993, despite not securing the full amount of finance, but still managing to break into new markets, our turnover doubled within six months. The real problems of underfinancing hit. We went back to the industry, to talk to spe-cific partners, to express our deep concern that if unable to refinance we would soon not be able to trade. Outside help came in on a contingency basis to help us seek our financial requirements and many of the buyers paid heavi-ly in advance in order to see us trade through.

During that year, and perhaps partially due to the enormous amount of pressure that both the success and the underfinancing of the company had caused, Ron (at the time financial director of the company) became ill.

In 1994 Caroline, having run the company almost single-handedly for the previous year, decided that more radical and innovative action needed to be taken. We went about floating the company on the mini Stock Exchange, a ruling at that time called the 4.21. A condition of this was that the first £150,000 was to be underwritten by the industry in order to secure the bal-ance needed. The consensus among our advisers in the City was that we could justify raising £1 million.

Failing to find a single partner to underwrite the full amount meant approaching a number of parties. Each in turn, directly or indirectly, expressed concern about stepping on the others' toes, and a failure to grasp how politics might snooker our future foiled our last big-scale attempt to refinance ourselves. This whole process took six months: to raise genuine interest, establish nervousness and then see the concept fail. During 1994 I had to virtually give up designing to concentrate on meetings and proposals to get the company back on a footing that would allow me to become a designer again. We simply believed that the 'winging it' from season to season approach was a waste of energy and that we could only go forward with medium-term security.

Through a friend in the industry, we were introduced to a firm of accountants with first hand experience at raising capital for designers. Neville Russell and specifically John Mellows displayed an instant and total belief that we had something positive to sell. Under certain conditions we set about selling the brand, the copyright of which belonged to me personally. In March 1995, the official value placed on the company was £1.5 million.

After trying so hard and in so many different ways, Caroline's and my belief in ourselves was at times very low. Despite these moments, the 'right' people always believed that there was a deal out there to be done. When an Italian cheque for a significant amount owed to us bounced, we were finally given notice by NatWest bank: we had a further six weeks. In effect, we stopped trading while there was an all-out blitz to find a buyer who would honour the creditors and take the brand forward to its full potential. On the eve of our deadline day, a deal with a 'feisty' gentleman from 'up north' fell through when it became clear that the creditors would get nothing, Caroline and I would be salaried employees and, once again, there was no real sense that they knew how to develop a brand. In reality, worth means nothing more than what someone is prepared to pay.

On 8 June at three-thirty and by mutual agreement with NatWest, the receivers were appointed and our staff were made redundant over a four-week period. After a long and hard battle, the consensus was that the company could go no further.

The press during this time were tremendous and I worked hard, as if at the height of post-show interviews. Many of them I had spoken to only weeks before about the bare bums in our last collection, *Edith's Sisters* (Autumn/Winter 1995). I now spoke to them about the grounding and banishing of our own. I felt their sympathy and it was as a direct result of their extensive coverage that the business got its best chance of finding a new opportunity to go forward.

The appointed receivers were not how I'd imagined they would be but were everything I could possibly have wished for. They were a family concern. Our Lady was a strident mix of Miss Marple and Shirley Williams; Our Man was a human fighter of right against wrong; and the Son Of could spot the gloating and vindictive from the first 'h' in 'hello' and had a healthy suspicion of grey shoes.

In total there were about thirty-five responses to the receivers and we started out determined to go through each one and assess it for its positives and negatives. Caroline went away for a short break and I carried on going into the office to meet the candidate faces for our possible future.

On day two of the receivership a gruff Indian voice spoke to me down the phone, saying that he'd like to buy me for £50,000 and no questions asked. Many of the approaches at the outset were very strange. None was stranger than a very large American who turned up two hours after the announcement and as a result of reading an article in the *Daily Telegraph*. He claimed he had part financed the Channel Tunnel and came in looking more like someone who had built it. We sat around our meeting table. He was huge and straddled his chair as he might do a horse.

Inexplicably challenged by him, I proceeded to tell him all the reasons why we should be backed. He had with him a sweaty Dickensian accomplice who took notes, grinned and laughed when prompted. All the way through, he kept one hand on his balls. I found him mesmerizing. Through our years of trade I have become familiar with the need to understand the thinking behind the 'suits'. In our time, I have met a few fine and extraordinary ones. Bombarded with them during the receivership, it is not so much the suit as the tie that now remains symbolic of this period. The tie: a silken, limp, patterned phallus most often worn in those professions where the spine of a man is deliberately hard to judge. Before me was a man who lived and breathed the Dow-Jones, a spine who had left all human qualities splattered somewhere over his first mega and dud deal.

The meetings went on, a juggling act of anything up to five heavies a day. I kept a file of all the opportunities and characters we met, giving the same speech in the translation that only money can understand. Exhausted, I was selling a designer in shock and feeling constantly braced, not knowing from where the next creditor blow might fall.

In the absence of good cash flow, a rampant disease in our trade, it is often the personal one-to-one skills that replace prompt payment in order to carry on. This was another way it was hard to divorce the company from the people. The many similarly sized set-ups that had stuck by us so generously during the illness year and since were the very ones who would now suffer because of our blazing commitment to trade through it. We felt sick at the unfairness of it all.

Receivership by its very nature is an advert to alert birds of prey to a fresh kill and we met many well-intentioned yet dishonest men. The path through perceived failure to the ledge just above is a slow one, and deals we might have accepted only a few years ago were not in touch with the real world as it is; they were simply more of the same. Once through the part of the receivership that required the directors' attentions, we went into full swing, talking and whittling down the possible routes that we could follow. This was the start of a period which, as I sit today, marks a full year since I designed anything at all. As time went by, the 'white walls' period came to visit me most mornings. From being surrounded by people, suddenly there was no one. Hand-packing up each department's office was like burying a string of old friends, one after the other. Work half finished was chucked and the fabric research for the next season binned. On the day we handed over the keys to the shop and office, the place was empty bar one room full of empty files.

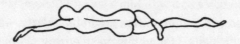

On this side of the eleven years I can now see how entrenched our last three were. Every day of the week had started with a print-out of the bank overdraft from NatWest, a computerized sheet outlining how much over our limit we were, and so began the horror of another day's dancing on nothing. It was perhaps a sign of our conscience and emotional pull into the business that paying others was always put before chasing the money owed to us. Our business was export-led; 85 per cent of our debts had to be chased abroad. A factoring policy hastily withdrawn from us in 1994, with only a week's notice before shipping a season, made collecting money an out-of-hours hassle. It took phenomenal courage to do what Caroline did each day – each creditor wanting payment, imagining that they were the only one. Caroline struck up some close and exhausting relationships in order to keep the thing moving. She dipped in a part of her soul and most of her personal self-esteem to fill that wretched gap called cash flow.

Now that there is time to think, it is as if we did none of it then. We clung on to each other, as many times it was all we had. Having taken the decision to trade through Ron's illness, in part because it was his wish – and it is ironic that we were profitable for that year – it was from that moment on a business torn through by both emotion and potential. The same energy to fight the disease went into keeping the company going. Caroline defined her role as protecting the part of the world that Ron strove to come back to and to that extent went through the same process that I did. I saw my role in life as being a two-way messenger, bringing news of the outside world to Ron, relaying it as one would hot gossip, then going straight back to the office and Caroline to cry and replay all that was horrifying, overwhelming and ever-changing.

We had intensive care of our own during this time, as Chris Lowrie from Pridie Brewster became our virtual full-time hand-holder. He put a structure to the chaos that had got even worse after Ron left. Henry and Riz, two financial assistants, were brought in to keep our books up to date. On the professional advice that we could, in pure and cold corporate terms, continue, we did, with as much focus on the day-to-day as on the continued saga of refinancing.

The quality of the individuals and companies who approached us with a view to investment during the receivership was as depressing as it had been among those we saw before it. The lack of knowledge in this country around brand-building and what it takes is appalling. It was as if the majority of the companies were looking either to give the mundane our edge or to commercialize it to such an extent that there was little reason to ask me to do it in the first place.

The few British success stories – Paul Smith and Ghost – in the designer market-place are not forged from the onset through the strength of long-term partnerships, as in Italy, France and Germany, but through maverick and focused individuals who push uphill, seemingly on their own, over many years. The unharnessed and wasted talent here is predominantly a result of fear and a lack of knowledge. The word 'design' in this country still to this day means risk, temperament and erratica. For all the partnerships that have been attempted, the lonesome route is most often purchased back by or dumped on the individual talent three to four seasons later.

The bigger group has trouble with the smaller division: expectations are often too high too soon, and the criteria for success on a large scale cannot so simply be applied to a small but growing concern. Many, although not all, of the associations forged between 'young designer' and manufacturer and large company have come a cropper through the destiny of the larger corporate body. When times are lean and a-changing, all the great and good inevitably go back to the ground they know best. The right finance married to a lack of vision and inexperience at brand-building, and the experience with no capital to back it up, were the most common situations encountered.

Neville Russell continued to pursue and negotiate opportunities as they arose. The last of them, in 1995, despite taking three months to work through and having my name written all over it, fell through yet again, twenty-four hours before signing.

Many of my conclusions about our industry are drawn from the sense of waste I have increasingly carried around with me. Privileged to have been trained in Italy, where fashion design works both creatively and as a business, I remain astonished and yet determined to find out why it is so hard to duplicate that success here, given that we breed it.

In my career only 10 per cent of my working time has been devoted to designing. At times I have marvelled that there ever was a perception of the Helen Storey name at all. On my first day of signing on the dole, a girl came up to me and asked me for my autograph. Once the scribble was over, we looked at each other, the uniqueness of the venue puzzling us both. Unable to make any sense of my feelings, I turned away and, staring ahead, started to think of the future. 'Next, please.'

13

Walking

the

Plank

Fashion is how we see ourselves. Whether it is important to us individually or not, it is our unspoken language. In our chosen skin we reveal our status, our state of mind. Uniquely in Britain, our designers frontline change, take the risk, make the initial mistake. In fearlessly celebrating instinct in a way few others are prepared to or can, they reflect life itself.

I think of British fashion design companies as rafts. Afloat in ingenious ways, we take blows and calms individually, often imagining they are aimed specifically at us. Not everyone comes out of art school, college or university wanting to set up in business on their own. Compared with my coming out, there are relatively few. However, for the annually brave and motley crew, I suggest there may be something we quite timelessly share.

From the day that as children we lose our abstract qualities for the pre-occupation of self-conscious decision, there is little in the educational process to give an artistic child a sense of their place in the world, or indeed the prospect of a job. In my nowhere years as a teenager, there were few opportunities to feel good at much. My late arrival and deep personal relief at finding I was good at 'something' set me on a path that was enough in itself. The very qualities which struck discord with me at school were the ones that beckoned me forward when I was attempting to build a business around my early and ragged creativity. Rarely do young, creative people, once given the opportunity to use their gifts, turn away from the challenge. Educated primarily in design, these young people are strong-armed into becoming mediocre marketeers, financiers and strategists on the signing of the first overdraft facility. In fashion design partnerships, it is rare that one of the partners is disinclined to design. More common is a shared and complementary vision to do it exclusively. From the beginning, therefore, half the equation for potential success is missing.

There is no commercial mechanism which allows a young fashion designer to secure finance ahead of time. Under-capitalization is our constant plague. The building starts alone and is highly personal. In this sense, to start up in the business of fashion in Britain is in fact not based on a blueprint which will give it the best chance; more, it is propelled forward through drive and passion alone.

Investment in oneself is inevitable. With no track record, there is no business unless secured early on by family and friends. From the outset, a fashion design company is emotionally charged, as if it were a new member of the family. The ability to see it with the degree of independence needed to make cold, corporate decisions is greatly hampered by the will to survive at any cost.

Two other areas have come to be considered as supplementary finance; in the absence of the real thing, they appear under the guise of income. These opportunities arise once a company's identity has started to take some marketable shape. The first of these is sponsorship. My partner, Caroline Coates, realized early on that fashion as a barometer of our times could as a marketing tool be of great value to other industries. Sponsorship has been made possible through the public's perception that our industry is a glamorous one, and can therefore reach a wide female market. Caroline's skill has always been to locate a genuine and mutually legitimate opportunity and explain it to another industry who might find the workings of ours foreign. Fashion sponsorship, although pioneered by people like Caroline, still has a long way to go. There is no reason why the long-term relationships forged between, say, sportswear manufacturers and sporting personalities cannot also flourish in our industry, a form of covert and commercial patronage. During our time, Caroline procured successful sponsorship deals between the Helen Storey name and many leading brands, to name a few, Alfa Romeo, BP, YKK Zips, Barclays Bank and Courtaulds.

The second form of finance is called consultancy. This can be dangerous to a small design company or it can be a lifesaver. Usually in year two or three of a designer's development approaches begin to emerge. These activities are taken on in good faith by both the designer and the manufacturer or retailer, but in reality only add to further confusion over what the designer market really is. The monetary rewards range from insulting to considerable for the few. Bereft of the capital and resources to commercialize our best ideas to the full, we have often given them away. We commit in the process a form of self-banishment into the further fields of experimentation and innovation. It is a pioneering land where there is little money to be made save giving back the idea a season later to bigger boys who appear to have the ability to print money.

As a nation, the instinct of big business has always been to use our inventors' works for its gain, rather than invest in them legitimately to ensure that the environment in which they were created survives. A more open and honest acknowledgement from the business community that part of the reason the innovative and the young go out of business so often is that their unpaid experimentation is ultimately on behalf of others. The independent designer is in fact fuelling the larger market-place at their own risk. There is a nationalistic laziness that silently and pompously assumes there will always be more talent ahead if the current names bite the dust. The cycle is unbroken because, bugger them all, it's true: we have a design education system which is superb but an outside climate which cannot turn that education into companies equipped to last the course.

The more common way of investing in our designers is for a larger company to support a smaller brand with the intention of adding volume to its existing core business. The investment in itself is not made in the belief that that smaller brand could become significant in its own right. By contrast, in Italy or Japan, the positioning of a designer next to financial and manufacturing clout is instinctive and makes commercial sense. It is rooted in the experience that brand-building takes years and for its full potential to be reached must have exclusive and constant attention in its formative years. Moreover, the handwriting that defines it should be commercialized for its benefit, and not diluted for others'.

We as designers subscribe to a uniquely creative insurance policy. Simply, in our success at failure, we never stop trying to succeed. The larger industry depends on this dynamic within us, for when called upon, it serves as a transfusion into a from time to time stagnant market-place. The danger in the consultancy route is that, in terms of research and development, we as designers are on the whole doing it for free, for if our services are successful, we in turn court the possibility of destabilizing our own customer base.

In any other industry that invests so highly at the education stage, we could not justify such a consistently miserable return. To accept the same level of failure in our lawyers, doctors and accountants would be unthinkable. In areas such as science, medicine and communications, there would be concerted efforts to keep the R&D child alive. It is capable of delivering tomorrow. While independent designers need more investment and wise guidance, they should always be considered as businesses. They are neither charities nor hobbies for the wife of a bloke with a bit of dosh.

It is a shame that our young designers, equipped on the whole to do just that, are still out there on the loose, expected to run companies as well. It should be accepted that designers should not be running the day-to-day or even, for that matter, any other area of the business other than design. To suggest that to do so is somehow the measure of true worth is to trick our most precious assets into at best a cruel diversion and at worse to fail. Our best chance of success as designers, over and above sensible investment, lies in partnership with another who by definition cannot do what we do and, perhaps as importantly, does not want to.

The current defining of a market-place for British fashion designers here is easy: it is those areas that the high street does not touch. We occupy the edge, appropriately named, for out on it there is little money to be made. The other area of scope is glamour and occasion-wear. True glamour needs considerable quality and fit to be convincing, so it is not surprising that few high-street chains can afford to invest in the minute detail of individual bodies. Few big names can justify a commitment to those seasons that keep some British designers alive: those Ascot and Henley moments, the wedding and barmitzvah, and what would we do without our balls? The two lessons to be drawn from the above – conclusions that, I imagine, any designer in business would endorse – are these: to set up in business without firsthand experience within the industry is creative suicide, and the strength of the home-market for non-designer products makes exporting essential. The creating of a defined marketable image is key to expanding abroad, as is the media's help in its identification.

The media and the promotion of our sector have a large part to play, as do we in our decision that the catwalk is how we wish to display our work. In the absence of any advertising budget that could be sustained, the catwalk is still the fastest and cheapest way to get images of one's products across the world. But it is the commitment to do a catwalk show that can most powerfully reshape and divert the energy of a young design company. The impact on a young designer when an event is successful or hyped is intoxicating to the point of danger. In part, I see the catwalk as an applauding of the part of our psyche long undiscovered or misplaced in years previous to success. Judgement can sometimes be impaired. At times we end up designing for it instead of that other plodding surface, the pavement. Perhaps designers and journalists should now be questioning why we walk this plank, and whether there isn't another way of doing the same job.

As a culture we love to poke fun at this industry. It can be with a contained respect, the attempt being to make coherent what, by its very British nature, is chaotic – to the extreme of the media trashing London Fashion Week *en masse*. The bulk of the fashion press, as dictated largely by a higher male editorial presence, has only two hemlines – up or down. In reporting the serious business of fashion, but then treating it at editorial level as one would a seasonal beauty contest, much important debate is continually ignored.

The promoting of our sector can be viewed similarly through the award system. Awards are important. To acknowledge arrival at a level of excellence, no matter where one is in one's career, is a positive thing. But to give the world outside the impression that all is well with us lot is unhelpful. At times we designers have shared little more than sequins for security and yet received validations for businesses barely there on the nights of the bestowed honour. What are we honouring? The image or the business which secures its projection. If we continually drive these two apart by celebrating that which is not there, we discourage any rectifying of the fundamental problems of the survival of our youngest companies.

To be aware of the problems and spout them in isolation is neither positive nor enough. Between Caroline and me there is a quarter of a century's experience. Along the way we have encountered numerous challenges that remain unresolved. These problems are ongoing and affect start-up businesses as well as those that have been around for a while.

The solutions sought are not intended to create an artificially 'easy ride' for independent designers. Beyond fair measures which lay the foundations to give any business the best chances of flourishing, every design company will ultimately stand or fall, destiny permitting, on its own abilities.

I have tried to clarify the climate in which British fashion designers find themselves trading, and also to suggest that inadvertently we have been 'setting them up', by encouraging creativity at the expense of equipping those with it for the real world, both in Britain and beyond. In addition, though, the 'real world' has some changing to do too.

The changes will take great courage and energy; but that is not enough. Most important of all is the perception of our role by those best able to help us. If we can accept that the aim is to rise above the notion that British independent designers are promoted as a PR exercise for the greater industry behind them, then there is scope for the future. It is broadly acknowledged that fashion is as socially and culturally important as music, film and, to some extent, the visual arts. There needs to be a recognition that fashion design at the cutting edge in Britain can create jobs, wealth and exports. The benefits that this sector can bring go far beyond its obvious role as advertisement. In turn, we as designers must give up the dream that our message in a bottle, aimed at a government door, will ever have a positive effect. One of the problems here is that at government level we have no specific door. While the DTI may be a good sounding-board for the everyday, their practical role goes little further than that. In my experience, the remit of the DTI is so broad that specific areas of grief cannot be fully and meaningfully addressed.

The mid-season anger of our ad hoc and talented crowd is as seemingly endless as the legitimate problems which face us. If we summarize our dilemmas they fall broadly into three categories: manufacturing, people and finance. In all these sectors there are dynamic people who can help to sort out our problems, and a think-tank is needed to plan some action, as is the commissioning of a feasibility study to look at the key and historically common problems. An action plan and working party drawn from informed people within the sector will be needed to put some of these findings into practice. Years one to five are crucial, and a strategy outlining all the highs and lows of that period would enlighten many from a very early stage. The moves to undertake such a study are currently underway.

In terms of manufacturing, the rising of a lone star in the north took the shape of Sally Smith from Coats Viyella. She has pursued her initiative to help designers manufacture their orders here in the UK with supreme vigour. This formula, however, needs company. One brilliant initiative is not enough, and without addressing the other key issues for designers, support of this nature runs the risk of inheriting as many problems as it solves. The British designer has two choices: to go the route of the 'special' or develop all-year-round business of meaningful volume which can then justify the input of a larger manufacturing force. Key to a designer's medium- and long-term success is a manufacturing relationship as patient and willing to grow as any financial one.

Success in fashion design is dependent on other people apart from the designer. A marriage bureau to match design, marketing, finance and management skills together from an early stage would be of great help. Education in these areas of expertise takes place in isolation; workshops to bring the players together before the end of their courses would allow a crucial swapping of skills for what it takes to design, market and sell through a fashion idea. Before a designer embarks on the setting up of a label, there must be an understanding of basic business skills and a willingness to work with them in the commercial world. The working party could explore the idea of patronage for the first five years of a designer label. Patronage need not be solely a commitment to cash but could take the form of people, skills and guidance. A willingness to underwrite the early years of finance would help the crucial defining years of a business. We raise significant sums of money for the promotion of our new names, but extending this laudable effort to the businesses behind them should not be seen as charity. There is a role for a new and general body to monitor (or an added dimension to an existing one) such patronage, assessing individual businesses for the next stages and pointing out appropriate investment routes. Patronage should be temporary and beyond the early stages of defining your market the business concerned should function independently.

There is a need for designers to re-establish their market-place in the face of the great success of high-street merchandise. The number of outlets capable of placing orders in the UK with independent designers fluctuates around the fifty mark. Opportunities to go straight to retail for the designers themselves could be re-examined. Own-retail allows far greater flexibility in a product's pricing. By remaining in the arena of wholesale exclusively, we render ourselves middle-men, our products incurring another's mark-up before reaching the consumer. This process means that our products will, I believe, always be overpriced. With the correct infrastructure, designers taking on the retail option could result in a price drop of anything up to 50 per cent and still leave a decent margin. I am not suggesting that there should be a rush to the high street by all designers, but given favourable lease conditions, offering the public the choice of buying the genuine article at a far lower price must be a worthwhile consideration. The reclamation of our market-place cannot be done with base-rate reductions alone. We must examine how we are getting to our customer. Without the backbone of a business in place on day one, this topic is often left to circumstance. With the thin retail base available to us and our inclination towards wholesaling exclusively in the UK, our potential for growth in the home market is stunted.

The nervousness of the financial institutions towards our sector is long established. On the whole, the banks' experience of the fashion industry is located in the ragtrade. The philosophy, management and upfront nature of a designer-built brand are still largely rooted in foreign soil. The designer is rarely the one to instil a sense of security into our friendly bank manager. While on occasions we have looked like a glamorous possibility, the changing nature of our product (compared with nails or screws) and the competition at high-street level only endorse further a sense of risk. Over my eleven continuous years in business, the most common off-the-record comment from the money lenders has been, 'Why do you do it?' They will never understand and I have occasionally wondered.

What is clear is that the presentation of this part of our sector needs translation. As each designer in turn reaches the stage where investment is needed to carry on, the same sporadic search among the same faces commences as if for the first time. Resistance to financing companies founded around innovation is not in any way restricted to fashion design. Our national hesitancy feels as profound as the outpouring of our ideas and missed opportunities. Communication is what is missing. Once again, this new organization perhaps initially sponsored by the industry and part-funded by the government could pool, package and present young designer businesses to a pre-targeted audience in a way that designers might find hard to do. In turn, beyond the start-up phase, a percentage of the finance raised could fund the ongoing running costs of the bureau itself. Without knowing the about legalities of such an idea, it appears to me that in the many fields in which Britain excels – from furniture design to film-making – there are many individual, isolated and time-consuming forays into the world of investment. Application to this organization might also be a moment to recognize legally whether an individual has a quality or idea worthy of copyright. The openness of this recognition, through whatever chosen network, to announce the designer as an investment opportunity, might also deter others from making unauthorized use of their designs.

The funding generally required to get a business past start-up and into the next phase falls, on the whole, through the investment gap. Neither small enough for grants or overdrafts to cope with and not big enough to interest the City and its offshoot players. The finance required is broadly below the £1 million mark and, as such, is seen as a something and nothing sum to those most able to invest. It is at this point that many of our talents (whose education has been paid for in Britain) leave the country to go to a climate more confident in the knowledge that British fashion can make money. They gain, we lose. Britain's instinct as an island is replicated in the formation of numerous others: small, independent business entities seemingly incapable of growing into the fashion empires found on the Continent. The irony of this condition is that although our talents spontaneously grow here, they are not tangibly valued. The climate for true creativity exists through continually quashing its best chances of survival. In sharp contrast, in a country like Italy, virtually devoid of art schools and trained fashion talent anywhere near the scale prevalent here, there are few home-grown heirs to inherit their thrones. Each of us has what the other wants. We have the creative input, they have muscle and a history of success in fashion.

If the objective is export-led, and by that I mean we acknowledge that our role as an island is to educate solely and package our designers for another country's use, why don't we just say so? Without making changes in our system, we have no justification for sadness when and if our designers go out of business.

There is a process in our industry called stone-washing. New unbroken garments are tossed *en masse* into a giant machine filled with stones, grit, chemicals and water. Any weak seams or faulty stitching leads to a frenzied shredding, a torn carnage bare hands would find hard to perpetrate. Those that make it through are prematurely aged but recognizably more saleable. The market-place for British designers is not dissimilar. We all pass through the same machine no matter what our talent, the treatment unsympathetic to an individual approach. A collective willingness to reconsider and aid this sector does exist. That quality on which designers risk their livelihoods could be as potent in the hands of those who do not design. Now, before this new generation is let down, is the time for the system to be made as creative as our disparate, floating crafts.

14

Outer
Space

We are right up the arse of us now; fashion has become a thing of the past. Now fully pillaged, it is kept alive in the hands of a genius or two, but on the whole we slide mish-mash-like towards the millennium. The power and commercial success of retrospective fashion is highly dependent on the current generation not having been around the first time. With the eighties threatening to be revived, the nineties are showing themselves as a decade of cleansing retaliation. The last few years of this century appear to be preparing a minimal canvas upon which we can expect the new. Sitting on the side of the fashion pool, I watch how we designers have been defining the future. On the whole, grappling with the just out of reach has been a styling exercise only.

In my hands and those of others, an instinctive need to move ourselves forward has been attempted by shifting backwards to relive a film made in 1968. The silver, white, plastics and synthetic shine of Stanley Kubrick's *2001: A Space Odyssey* was the broadest influence on designers, stylists, videos and magazines in the early nineties. An era made famous as the designer decade has not been about true design at all but about the stylist.

The future for independent designers functions on two levels. The first is what their place in it will become and the second, which will determine the first, is what that product will need to look like to ensure there is a future for real designers at all. At present, we designers have lost not so much our nerve as our place.

You cannot afford to ask yourself if the world needs another of your collections when your life is on the proverbial line, when your staff depend on you for their livelihood or when you believe that the next one could be the best yet. The world seems to be talking to us, but there are too many of us with too little to say. As designers, we cannot compete with the technology available to the giants. In this sense the future is expensive. The investment and time needed to fully develop the 'new', whether in fibre or in yarn, can be commercially justified only when the end user can order it by the ton. There is a shop called Egg and it stands as white to the black of the big boys, the multinational chainstores. Independent designers will have to come up with something unique to survive; accept a pull towards innovation, even though the risk is that their products may be too advanced for their customers and not sell in large enough numbers at the outset to support the infrastructure within which they were made. We have no choice, however, but to produce goods worthy of our antique shops of tomorrow: something possibly unproduceable in bulk, back to a craft with pride; not couture as it stands, but a product which reflects a unique hallmark of an individual designer, a uniqueness which need not necessarily drive the price. Today's young designers must consider where their edge lies and, if it is remotely blurred, should consider sharpening it. For me this much-needed quality has already partially emerged, but for now it is located in the small. It dresses the furthest north, south, east and west of a woman – her edges, her finishing touches. One can find it in the hats of Philip Treacy, in the shoes of Manolo Blahnik and among our jewellery designers. The loudest noise in our industry's recent history has been the whisper and tight snap of a handbag clasp. A bag by Prada has signified that the power of dressing women in the nineties lies not in a total look for her every waking moment but in the 'special' about her – snatches of time that, by definition, cannot last long.

The problem for us is a big one. It may lie somewhere in the falsity of the ongoing aim. A designer educated in the seventies and early eighties would have aimed high, thought big. I did. What I saw from Moschino and Gaultier looked achievable from behind my college table. But the climb up from idea to empire is colossal. With good reason the British high street's ability to do their job, and also some of ours as well, demands that we face this dilemma now. With the changing climate for independent designers and the rare circumstances in this country, where development, finance and brand-building expertise align, it is only a question of time before the already brutally restricted budgets for education will be further challenged.

So what of all these talents which need nurturing? How do we select them on day one? How do we judge what will make good fodder for the corporation? Who will be the wild card of tomorrow? Why don't we train buyers, merchandisers and pattern-cutters on the same scale as we do designers? What hope for the creative if to follow an art course now demands that one takes chemistry at the same time?

The future is as much a place for industry and the supporting services to reconsider their input into designers as it is for the designers themselves to contemplate their relevance. The enemy is not the media or the system in isolation. The real enemy is far harder to criticize. It is me, you, the designers, as we continue to strive to survive at any cost to our living, our relationships and occasionally our health.

In conclusion, the fate of the independent designer rests in a number of places. First, with the designers themselves, to develop a market internationally, and a product distinct from the mainstream competition. Second, with investment in terms of resources and cash, to be directed as much to the building and sustaining of the businesses as it is currently to the promotion of them. Lastly, with a form of 'Bible', created to deter young businesses from making the same mistakes as their predecessors.

For me the future is about finding a new relevance for my passion to design. Creativity in my hands need not belong exclusively to fashion. Rightly or wrongly, the boundaries between the 'art' sectors seem to be blurring. Excitement in fashion, as I define it, may soon be found when applied outside the industry. The fashion designer pure must find a new home somewhere between the land of couture and science. The inevitable consequence of an era where progress has been synthetically generated is that in place of the pure, a hybrid medium, a cross-fertilization of many art forms, will take us cataclysmically into the millennium: artists as film-makers, singers as artists, actors as painters, furniture designers as sculptors.

It may be a while before we move out of the creative darkness we are in at the moment, years before the art of painting is bigger news than any price it may command, before ideas come rather than being generated. We've got classic, we've seen modern, we've felt minimal, reality is only virtual. In the absence of nature, manufactured is now real. Hell will come the day when a machine can 'feel' and, in the meantime, I'm going back to my egg.

If I look at the things that matter to me, they span from children to sweeping leaves; from art in its broader sense to feeling the sun. Success in the past meant rarely having to queue; in queues since I have contemplated my next move. A test of any great friendship is how it survives change. In mine with Caroline, made dynamic through work and impassioned through an illness, still alive when both have passed, the future is now unfolding itself into a partnership of new ideas. If we were anything in business, then we were creators of these, but this time it must be simpler, must be nearer the reason for doing it, must house some of our qualities that were homeless in the company of old. The formation of a partnership to launch the first idea came after successive deals and offers either fell through or held no long-term potential. In its precise form here, it outlines a concept which indicates the motivation behind our future work together.

I feel I have forever moved between places where others were so sure – a messenger and an interpreter of ways and unquestioned instincts. In my work, in my relationships, I have no sense of end or of what is coming. A pen hits a page and a process starts. If I try to control it, as I often do, something is lost. If I try to explain it before it is finished, it vanishes. I know the brief, I sense the person and from then on anything can happen. I never arrive. I am always on the way.

The first sunrise of the millennium will be on Caroline Island in the Pacific at 5.43 GMT. I can already feel a media-provoked build-up, but also a subconscious one independent of it. The sun will come up and we, in staggered formation, after it. In me it already serves as a summit. Towards it, a race to negotiate more peace, to cure another disease, and from its top, to look back over what we have created and weigh it against what we insist on destroying. In reality it may, of course, make no difference at all. We cannot rely on it to change anything: only perhaps note a moment when we acknowledge whether we have changed at all. Just another waking moment, one more cup of tea.

The Helen Storey Trust

The Concept
To establish an organization or 'trust' which brings the work of Helen Storey to the consumer; where all profits and some income is passed on to a coterie of charities. The organization would employ staff in design, administration, retail and management.

The Charities
From day one the 'trust' would work in partnership with charities; the success of the enterprise is reliant on their support and involvement. We have to date the formal endorsement of the Helen Storey Trust from two international and three national charities.

Key Features
* For the first time to bring a designed clothing product to the consumer at a totally affordable price, up to 70 per cent cheaper than normal.

* To create a unique partnership between a designer and charities, a totally non-commercial framework where profits are for good causes rather than corporate profit.

* The 'trust' would actively develop the skills of women, especially those returning to the workforce after raising a family, by training those in education and the recently graduated, the long-term unemployed and disadvantaged, and by providing flexible part-time work for management and workers.

* To be at the cutting edge not only of design but also of the way in which funds are raised for charities that are also of benefit to the consumer.

* To create a new and modern framework for corporate sponsorship, particularly for the clothing sector, where any 'investment' could obtain tax relief.

Other Considerations

* A totally new concept with no known role models which will hopefully stimulate other ventures of this kind.

* Highly topical in view of recent attitudes towards charity; this alone will stimulate media interest.

* Of benefit to companies wishing to have a high-profile charity fashion involvement.

* A job creator: it is envisaged that at least five part-time management posts can be created, up to twenty training posts per annum and twenty other part-time jobs.

* An opportunity to harness the considerable skills of the instigators in an exciting framework with much scope for development.

* It is our wish to launch the 'trust' formally in the autumn of 1997, although its activities will begin informally in September 1996 at the launch of *Fighting Fashion*. The event will be dedicated to The Imperial Cancer Research Fund.

Acknowledgements

I'd like to thank the following people, who, in differing ways, made this book possible: Victoria Buxton at Faber, my father, Don, Liz , Ron and Caroline.